some experimental ideas for teachers

Wellington High School.

THE
SCHOOL
MATHEMATICS
PROJECT

computing in
mathematics

some
experimental
ideas
for teachers

CAMBRIDGE
AT THE UNIVERSITY PRESS 1971

Published by the Syndics of the Cambridge University Press
Bentley House, 200 Euston Road, London NW1 2DB
American Branch: 32 East 57th Street, New York, N.Y.10022

© Cambridge University Press 1971

ISBN: 0 521 08150 5

Printed in Great Britain by
Jarrold & Sons Ltd, Norwich

THE SCHOOL MATHEMATICS PROJECT

The Project was originally founded in 1961 by a group of practising school-teachers who believed that there were, at that time, serious shortcomings in traditional school mathematical syllabuses, and that there was a need for experiment aimed at developing new syllabuses which would reflect modern ideas and applications of mathematics.

The activities of the S.M.P. are, by now, well-known, as are its series of text-books – Books A-H for the main school, Books 1-5 and the Additional Mathematics Books for O-level, Advanced Books 1-4 and Further Mathematics Books for A-level. Full details of these publications and activities, and of teacher-training courses, are given annually in the current Director's Report which may be obtained on request to the S.M.P. Office, Westfield College, Kidderpore Avenue, London, NW3 7ST.

So much is, in a sense, past history. But the S.M.P. continues to look forward and to encourage a process of more or less continual change and updating of school mathematics teaching. Thus, among other things, it now turns its attention to the implications that computing power in the school classroom holds for mathematics.

Not enough is yet known about how computers can best be used in the classroom to illumine mathematical curricula: there is much exploratory work first to be done. The books of this new series – under the generic title *Computing in Mathematics* – therefore investigate various applications of computers to school mathematics, and it is hoped that, by provoking discussion over the next few years, they will help to prepare the ground for a more cohesive course in the future.

Finally it is particularly hoped that, as has been the case with previous S.M.P. books, teachers from all types of schools will send their comments and criticisms to the editors of these books.

BRYAN THWAITES
Director

Westfield College
January 1971

This is based on the original contributions of

B. H. Blakeley
M. I. Jones
A. E. Lawrance
Phyllis Starr
J. D. Tinsley

and has been edited by J. D. Tinsley and B. H. Blakeley.

Grateful acknowledgement is made of the help of all those teachers who submitted comments and criticisms of the draft version of this book.

The Project owes a great deal to its Secretaries, Miss J. Sinfield and Miss J. Try, for their assistance and typing in connection with this book.

contents

preface

This, the first book in the S.M.P. Computing in Mathematics series, is more of a collection of essays than a continuous text. The authors all have experience of teaching computing topics in school, and all believe that the computer will play a growing part in the teaching of mathematics; but no attempt has been made, at this early stage of the series, to grade the text so that it is aimed at any particular age or ability group. Indeed, experience has shown that many of the ideas in the text can be successfully introduced at a variety of levels. One of the important aspects of the use of the book will be an attempt, on a broad basis, to discover the stage in the pupil's development at which it is most appropriate to deal with the various topics.

The way in which the chapters have been written has been severely constrained by the knowledge that, at present, few schools have computing power in the classroom. But the number of schools with computing facilities is growing, and it is vitally important that teachers should prepare themselves for developments in this direction. The authors feel that teachers can, even now, incorporate into their mathematics teaching – whether on a traditional or 'new' syllabus – most of the ideas in this book. If it is possible for pupils to write programs and have them run on a computer, this can only add to the value of the work covered.

1 basic concepts

1.1 calculating devices in school

In recent years there has been an increasing tendency to use a variety of calculating aids in the classroom. Cuisenaire rods and Dienes multi-base blocks have become important in the teaching of arithmetic in primary schools; slide rules and desk calculating machines are to be found in many secondary schools. Much useful work can be based on a historical survey of calculating devices – for example, the abacus and Napier's rods – and on the work of Charles Babbage. Several texts are available which cover the use of these devices and explain their underlying mathematical properties (refs. 1, 2, 3, 4).

1.2 the basic concept of a computer

All the devices mentioned above carry out arithmetical operations and call for detailed manipulation. The electronic computer does not require such supervision but its actions must be carefully planned in a prepared program of elementary instructions. Once this program has been prepared, the computer can carry out long and detailed calculations without the intervention of an operator. Modern electronic engineering has made it possible for computers to perform such calculations at great speed and with a high degree of accuracy. In the classroom we can teach the method of preparing a problem for the computer, and this creates in the pupil an awareness that the machine is a servant whose actions are entirely predictable. In this book the main emphasis is upon the planning aspect, without reference to any particular machine.

Modern computing systems are highly complex but may be illustrated by simple models. Figs. 1 and 2 show how the actions of a clerk working at a desk compare with the functions of the components of a computer. Fig. 3 shows the correspondence between the two systems.

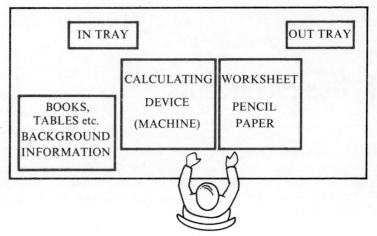

fig. 1

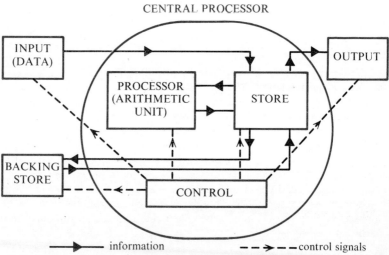

fig. 2

Pupils can act out these situations in a computer game. The program (or sequence of instructions) is given to a pupil who sits at a table in a position labelled Control. Four other pupils sit at the table in positions labelled Input, Processor, Store and Output respectively.

Input has an ordinary office in-tray which contains all the data relevant to the program. This set of data will be in the form of numbers, and each number will be given to Store when the appropriate instruction is read from the program by Control. Store has a box divided into cells which are clearly numbered (a set of pigeon-holes will do). Numerical calculations are performed by Processor, who is equipped with an ordinary desk calculating machine. Output has an office out-tray, paper and pencil.

The pupils taking part seat themselves in the correct positions round the table. A program is placed in front of Control with the associated data in the input tray. The program consists of a pile of cards, each containing a single instruction. Control hands the cards in sequence to the appropriate pupils at the table. On receiving a card, the pupil concerned carries out the instruction and returns the card to Control.

parts of system	human	electronic
Input	in-tray and lists of instructions	tape or card reader
Control	human brain	circuitry
Main store	pencil, paper (action tray)	core stores (magnetic)
Processor	paper, pencil etc.	circuitry (accumulator)
Backing store	books, etc.	magnetic tape, disc, etc.
Output	out-tray	punched card, magnetic tape, printed copy

fig. 3

Let us use this computer to multiply 4·5 by 3·1. The numbers 4·5 and 3·1 are written on separate cards and placed in the input tray. Control first gives to Input a card on which is written 'Put the next number into cell 1'. Input takes the top card from his tray and gives it to Store, who puts the card in the pigeon-hole labelled 1. The next instruction: 'Put the next number into cell 2' will again be carried out by Input. Both numbers are now in the storage cells, and the arithmetic operation (multiplication in this case) can now be performed. The next instruction card tells Store to pass the contents of cell 1 to Processor who sets this number (4·5) on the calculator. Two more cards are needed for the arithmetic operation. The first instructs Store to send the contents of cell 2 to Processor, and the second tells Processor to 'Multiply' the number on his calculator by the number (3·1) just received from Store. The result of the calculation is then sent back to Store by an instruction from Control. If cell 10 is used for the result, the next instruction Send the contents of cell 10 to Output will move the answer card (13·95) to the output tray, thus completing the program.

In fig. 2, solid lines represent the paths taken by information (data) and broken lines indicate the paths of the control signals. Pupils can easily 'design' their own 'machine' for running programs and one such game is shown in the film Man and Computer; A Perspective (ref. 5).

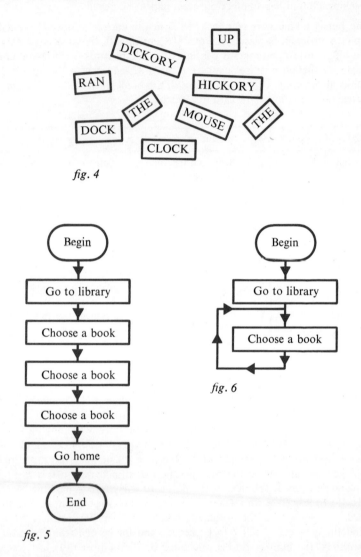

fig. 4

fig. 5

fig. 6

1.3 flow charts

Even young children will appreciate that the words in fig. 4 must be re-arranged into a logical order to provide a meaningful phrase or sentence. Similarly, a set of instructions must be arranged in a strict sequence if a desired action is to be achieved. A convenient way of illustrating this sequence is by means of a flow chart. Fig. 5 illustrates the set of instructions for a visit to the library. Fig. 6, however, is more concise and makes use of a loop. This diagram is obviously incomplete for some method is required of terminating the loop after a given number of books has been chosen. Questions to control this process have been introduced in fig. 7 and it should be noticed that there are only two possible answers to the questions asked: YES or NO.

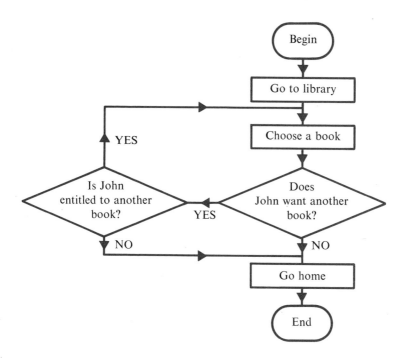

fig. 7

A computer programmer must have a clear and complete understanding of the problem to be solved. Drawing a flow chart is an excellent way of organising the necessary instructions and later chapters show how this is employed in a variety of situations.

Several school texts contain examples on the construction of flow charts (refs. 6, 9, 10, 11, 12, 13, 14) but one such chart is given in fig. 8. It represents the stages involved in converting six sets of measurements given in yards, feet and inches into metres and centimetres, correct to the nearest centimetre. This chart introduces the idea of a counter, to keep a record of the number of separate sets of measurements entered. The question Is counter=6? ensures that the process is carried out only six times. The instruction Correct result to nearest cm would need to be broken down into several simple steps, but this is left as an exercise for the reader.

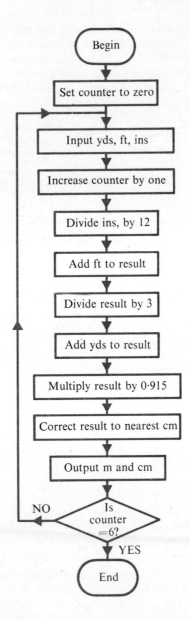

fig. 8

examples Construct flow charts for the following problems:

1 The Essempaeans are a race, inhabiting a part of North London, who have a straightforward taxation system. Tax assessment is based upon age. There are four rates of tax corresponding to the four age groups 0–18, 19–40, 41–60 and over 60. Write out in full the decision elements required to examine a given age and to branch to the appropriate tax rate.

2 Any two numbers are written down. Draw a flow chart to arrange the numbers in descending order.

3 Repeat question 2 for any three numbers.

4 Think of a number between 0 and 7 inclusive. By asking just three yes–no questions is it possible for someone else to find your number? Draw a flow chart incorporating the three questions.

1.4 number bases

Number-base work is not new to school textbooks: it was to be found in books published 100 years ago. Yet the work was seldom taught – perhaps there was no motivation – but the advent of the electronic computer has made it a commonplace topic in the school syllabus today. Since much has been written elsewhere about this subject we shall content ourselves with a few isolated, yet interesting, cases related to scales of notation and the binary system.

The cyclically permuted binary system deserves a mention. The columns are headed $(2^n-1) \ldots 15, 7, 3, 1$; and the symbols 0 and 1 are used. Reading from left to right, 1s are alternately added and subtracted. 0s are ignored, so that 1011 represents $+15-3+1=13$. The first few numbers are given below:

15	7	3	1	interpretation
			1	$1=1$
		1	1	$3-1=2$
		1	0	$3\ \ =3$
	1	1	0	$7-3\ \ =4$
	1	1	1	$7-3+1=5$
	1	0	1	$7\ \ -1=6$
	1	0	0	$7\ \ =7$
1	1	0	0	$15-7\ \ =8$
	etc.			etc.

Note that 15 would be 1000 and 16 would be 11000.

Thus only one figure has to be altered in going from 15 to 16, or in terms of electric switches, only one switch has to change its state. Compare this with the binary system where

$$15 \text{ is } 1111 \quad \text{and} \quad 16 \text{ is } 10000,$$

showing that five figures have to be altered in going from 15 to 16. In a computer circuit it would be necessary to change the state of five circuits or switches. Perhaps readers may be able to suggest some disadvantage of the above system.

Another project using the binary scale which might interest young pupils is one in which they are asked to produce four cards as follows:

> card *A* containing the numbers 1, 3, 5, 7, 9, 11, 13, 15;
> card *B* containing the numbers 2, 3, 6, 7, 10, 11, 14, 15;
> card *C* containing the numbers 4, 5, 6, 7, 12, 13, 14, 15;
> card *D* containing the numbers 8, 9, 10, 11, 12, 13, 14, 15.

Ask someone to choose a number from 1 to 15, but only to tell you on which cards it appears. From this information you should be able to tell him the chosen number. Pupils are interested to know why this works and can easily make a set of cards to contain numbers up to 63. How many cards will be needed?

'Russian Multiplication' also appeals to a class.

Two columns are used, each headed by one of the numbers involved in the multiplication. The process is carried out by repeatedly doubling the left-hand number and halving the right-hand number, ignoring remainders, e.g.

61	23
122	11
244	5
488	2
976	1

Now delete the lines where the right-hand number is even and add up the remaining left-hand numbers, in this case $61 + 122 + 244 + 976 = 1403$. Why does this work?

Write out the process again, expressing the number to be halved in the binary scale, e.g.

$$61 \times \{2^4 \times 1 + 2^3 \times 0 + 2^2 \times 1 + 2^1 \times 1 + 2^0 \times 1\}$$

Is it possible to multiply two numbers together by trebling the first, while dividing the second by three?

Another problem which might be investigated is subtraction by using a complement. On a calculating machine it can easily be shown that subtracting a number is the same as adding its complement. The complement of a number in base 10 is found by subtracting that number from a power of 10 equal to the number of digits the machine can hold. For example, if a machine works to four decimal digits, the complement of the number 326 is found as follows:

$$10000 - 0326 = 9674$$

This rule can easily be tested in a particular example:

$$\begin{array}{ccc} 1749 & & 1749 \\ -0326 & \text{is equivalent to} & +9674 \\ \hline 1423 & & (1)1423 \end{array}$$

The first 1 must be ignored, for it arises from the fact that we have added $(10000-0326)$ rather than subtracted 0326. In practice the leading digit will be lost because of the limited capacity of the machine.

In a computer, calculations are performed in binary arithmetic, but the same rule applies. Thus the 'two's' complement of 0010110100 is 1101001100. A comparison of these two numbers digit by digit from the right-hand end shows that they are the same up to and including the first 1; then a 1 in the number becomes a 0 in the complement and vice versa. If *every* 1 and 0 are reversed, the result is known as a one's complement and this type of complement can be readily produced by a machine. The reader will notice that a one's complement can be converted into a two's complement by adding 1. Subtraction may therefore be performed by adding the one's complement and then adding a 1 to the result.

As an example, subtract 59 from 158 on a machine with a capacity of eight binary digits. In binary, 158 is 10011110 and 59 is 00111011 (using all eight digits). The one's complement is 11000100.

$$\begin{array}{ll} & 10011110 \\ & 11000100 \\ \text{adding:} & (1)01100010 \\ \text{adding 1:} & (1)01100011 \end{array}$$

As before, we ignore the leading digit to give an answer of 1100011.

1.5 punched cards

The two-state system of Yes/No, Off/On, 1 and 0 can be demonstrated by the use of punched cards. Much interesting information about a class can be stored on punched cards and excellent illustration can be found in refs. 15 and 10. Punched cards may be purchased, but it is not too difficult to manufacture one's own in the school workshop by drilling through a pile of cards clamped between two metal sheets used as templates. Care should be taken, however, to prevent the cards from burning.

Fig. 9 shows a master card and a typical card from a set which can be used to store information about numbers. Each pupil in a class could be given a card from a set of thirty-six cards labelled consecutively 1–36, and told to cut the slots relevant to the number of the card he or she has, i.e. leave a hole if the number possesses the property recorded in that position.

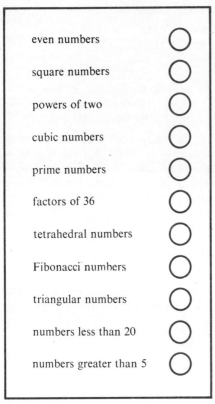

even numbers

square numbers

powers of two

cubic numbers

prime numbers

factors of 36

tetrahedral numbers

Fibonacci numbers

triangular numbers

numbers less than 20

numbers greater than 5

fig. 9

If the cards are now collected together, the stack may be sorted by using a knitting needle to pick out cards which have holes, rather than slots, in a particular position. (See ref. 8 for a further sorting experiment.)

1.6 matrix algebra

Many calculations in a computer reduce to the evaluation of sums of products, and matrices can be used to order and store numerical values before and after such calculations are performed. Many books give simple introductions to matrix algebra (refs. 7, 9) but a typical example is given below.

A nurseryman offers the following collections of trees for sale:

assortment *A* contains   two rose trees, one pear tree, two apple trees, one peach tree and two almond trees.

assortment *B* contains   one rose tree, one apple tree and one almond tree.

assortment *C* contains   two rose trees, one apple tree, one peach tree and one almond tree.

assortment *D* contains   two peach trees and two almond trees.

A customer orders three of assortment *A*, two of *B*, eight of *C* and one of *D* as presents for his friends.

The prices of each item are:

rose trees	£1·00 each	apple trees	£1·20 each
pear trees	£1·50 each	almond trees	£2·00 each
peach trees	£1·25 each		

Calculate the cost of the order.

The composition of the assortments can be expressed in matrix form as follows:

$$\begin{array}{c} \\ A \\ B \\ C \\ D \end{array} \begin{array}{ccccc} r & p & pch & ap & al \\ \begin{pmatrix} 2 & 1 & 1 & 2 & 2 \\ 1 & 0 & 0 & 1 & 1 \\ 2 & 0 & 1 & 1 & 1 \\ 0 & 0 & 2 & 0 & 2 \end{pmatrix} \end{array}$$

The order matrix is:

$$\begin{array}{cccc} A & B & C & D \\ (3 & 2 & 8 & 1) \end{array}$$

Hence the total order is:

$$\begin{array}{cccc} A & B & C & D \\ (3 & 2 & 8 & 1) \end{array} \begin{pmatrix} 2 & 1 & 1 & 2 & 2 \\ 1 & 0 & 0 & 1 & 1 \\ 0 & 0 & 2 & 0 & 2 \end{pmatrix} = \begin{array}{ccccc} r & p & pch & ap & al \\ (24 & 3 & 13 & 16 & 18) \end{array}$$

The cost matrix is: giving a total cost of:

$$\begin{pmatrix} 1·00 \\ 1·50 \\ 1·25 \\ 1·20 \\ 2·00 \end{pmatrix} \quad (24 \quad 3 \quad 13 \quad 16 \quad 18) \begin{pmatrix} 1·00 \\ 1·50 \\ 1·25 \\ 1·20 \\ 2·00 \end{pmatrix}$$

$$= (24 \times 1·00 + 3 \times 1·50 + 13 \times 1·25 + 16 \times 1·20 + 18 \times 2·00)$$
$$= £99·95$$

1.7 evaluation of formulae and the time factor

Many calculations can be classed as formulae evaluation. Consider the relationship (between miles and kilometres) expressed by $M = \frac{5}{8}K$. A single evaluation of *M* for a given value of *K* is not an arduous exercise.

If, however, we wish to convert a large number of values of *K* then a computer program written once only, but applied to each value in turn, would reduce the time involved and also the possibility of human error.

This, of course, assumes that the program is 100 per cent correct initially.

12

This last point emphasises the degree of concentration required in programming, because, as in so many other spheres, one can never be half right. One cannot, so to speak, get 70 per cent of the marks. The program must be 100 per cent correct, as one wrong instruction will ruin the whole of that program. The evaluation of M for some value of K is a problem from *School Mathematics Project, Book 1*, p. 183 and we can assign some times (in seconds) for completing each step as it is solved in that book. Using these arbitrarily chosen times, a flow chart of the operations can be drawn as in fig. 10.

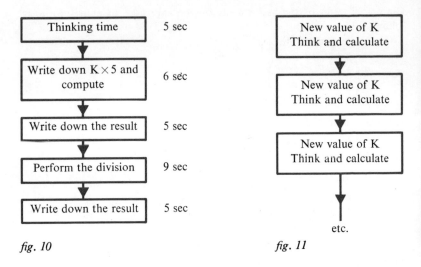

fig. 10   *fig. 11*

By choosing these artificial times, we have reached a situation in which the total thinking and writing times are the same. Fig. 11 illustrates the action of a human operator when performing the same calculation on a large number of different values of K.

With practice, a human operator may speed up slightly, but any gain in time is likely to be counteracted by fatigue. The amount of thinking and operating time is therefore about the same for each value of K.

With an automatic computing machine, the situation is quite different. The program must be prepared before any calculations can take place, and this task will probably take the programmer more time than if he were to perform a single calculation by hand. However, once the program is written, the human thinking time is finished, and fig. 12 illustrates the repeated application of the program to many different values of K.

Even if we assume that the time taken to perform one calculation is the same by both hand and automatic machine, there will be a certain number of calculations for which the total time taken is the same. For a greater number of calculations, the use of an automatic machine will prove to be the faster method.

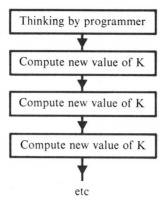

etc

fig. 12

This 'break-even' point will be investigated algebraically in the next example.

example A motorist observes that when he drives his car at certain speeds, his petrol consumption is as shown in the following table:

speed in km hour	(u)	50	70	90	110
petrol consumption in km litre	(c)	12	10	8	6

Rewriting this table of values in the form

u	50	70	90	110
10c	120	100	80	60

it appears that there is a relationship of the form:

$$u+10c=170,$$
$$\text{or } 10c = 170-u,$$
$$\text{or } c = 17 - u/10.$$

This formula gives the consumption of petrol in km per litre.
If the motorist travels a distance of d km we can see that he will use d/c litres of petrol.
Hence the number of litres of petrol (n) for a given distance is given by:

$$n=\frac{d}{17-u/10}$$

Assuming that it takes 5 seconds to write down a result, that initial thinking occupies some 5 seconds, divisions take 9 seconds, multiplications 6 seconds and subtractions 6 seconds, the calculation of values of n for given values of and d on a desk calculator would follow the pattern of fig. 13.

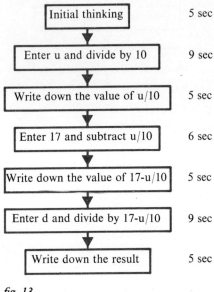

Initial thinking	5 sec
Enter u and divide by 10	9 sec
Write down the value of u/10	5 sec
Enter 17 and subtract u/10	6 sec
Write down the value of 17-u/10	5 sec
Enter d and divide by 17-u/10	9 sec
Write down the result	5 sec

fig. 13

Total operator writing and thinking time   20 sec
Total time the calculator is performing operations   24 sec

The times taken for this more lengthy calculation emphasise further the difference between fig. 11 and fig. 12. The programmer may have to spend more than 20 seconds in planning his program, but this time is shared amongst all the calculations performed.

We shall assume first that the times taken to perform a calculation automatically and by hand are the same, and that the programming time is the same as the manual thinking time. If there are N calculations to be made, the total time taken by desk calculating machine is $44N$ seconds. The corresponding time by automatic machine is given by:

$$(20+24N) \text{ secs}$$

The ratio between these times is given by the function:

$$y = \frac{44N}{20+24N}$$

which has been plotted in fig. 14. It can be seen from the graph that the ratio tends to a value of 44/24 as N increases, and that for a large value of N, this ratio is independent of the initial programming time. Thus the automatic machine is almost twice as fast as the desk machine when a large number of calculations are performed.

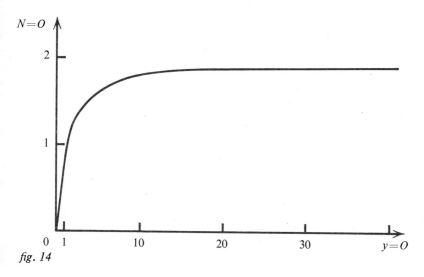

fig. 14

We shall now repeat the calculation for a more realistic set of timings. Assume that the programmer takes 20 minutes to prepare the program for an electronic computer, and that the computer takes $\frac{1}{10}$ of a second to evaluate the formula for a given value of K. As before, the time taken by desk calculating machine will be about 44 seconds.

Thus the total time for the desk machine is still $44N$ seconds, whereas the total time by computer is:

$$[20 \times 60 + N(1/10)] \quad \text{sec}$$

The ratio of these two times is given by:

$$y = \frac{\text{time by desk machine}}{\text{time by electronic computer}} = \frac{44N}{20 \times 60 + N/10}$$

$$\Rightarrow y = \frac{440N}{(12\ 000 + N)} = \frac{440}{\left[\dfrac{12\ 000}{N} + 1\right]}$$

When N is large, $\dfrac{12\ 000}{N} \to 0$ \qquad and so \quad $y \to 440$.

Thus for a large number of calculations, the computer is about 440 times as fast as the desk calculating machine.

The 'break-even' point, i.e. the number of calculations which must be performed before the use of a computer shows a saving of time, is when $y=1$. This occurs when the numerator and the denominator of the ratio are equal.

The corresponding value of N is given by:

$$440N = 12\ 000 + N$$
$$\Rightarrow 439N = 12\ 000$$
$$\Rightarrow \quad N = \frac{12\ 000}{439} = 27$$

This value of N implies that if we wish to calculate the number of litres of petrol used for 28 journeys at uniform speed, we should use the electronic machine if we require the results in a hurry.

1.8 counting the cost

The discussion in section 1.7 was based on the time factor, but it is also interesting to consider the comparative cost of performing a given calculation by hand and by computer. It may be thought that the computer is a very expensive device, but in practice the cost per calculation is much lower on a modern electronic machine than by any other method. This is because the computer can perform calculations at a very high speed, and the time taken on a particular job is measured in fractions of a second. High labour costs in industry and in commerce have made it imperative that management should take advantage of this relatively cheap device.

2 the computer

2.1 introduction

In this chapter we introduce a hypothetical computer which can be used to illustrate the basic concepts of programming as required by the mathematician. No such computer actually exists but the principles outlined below can easily be used to explain either the actions of a programmable calculator or the necessary steps which have to be taken when preparing a program for a full-scale computer. However, it has been found helpful to present such a conceptual machine so that pupils can have a model on which to base their thinking.

2.2 instructions and data

When playing the computer game described in chapter 1, pupils realise that a large number of basic instructions are required when the program for even a simple calculation is organised. In that game, the set of instruction cards was stored on Control's desk and the individual instructions were followed in sequence. An important fact to notice is that both instructions *and* data are held on cards, and that all the cards must be stored somewhere. In a real computer, instructions are stored in coded form and may occupy locations within the store similar to those used for items of data. In practice, both instructions and data are stored as patterns of binary digits, each pattern representing a simple instruction or an individual character, alphabetical or numerical.

2.3 the store

Consider the store of a hypothetical computer which consists of a large number of individual locations each of which can hold either a simple instruction or a number (fig. 1). We can refer to each individual storage location by means of an address, and the store can be thought of as a set of houses along a street. If our computer has 100 storage locations, we can use the two-digit numbers 00, 01, 02, ... 98, 99 to denote the addresses of the individual locations. Instructions are usually held in a particular part of the computer store and must be entered into store before the computation can be performed. The preparation of these instructions is known as *programming*, and the way in which the instructions are written is called a *programming language*.

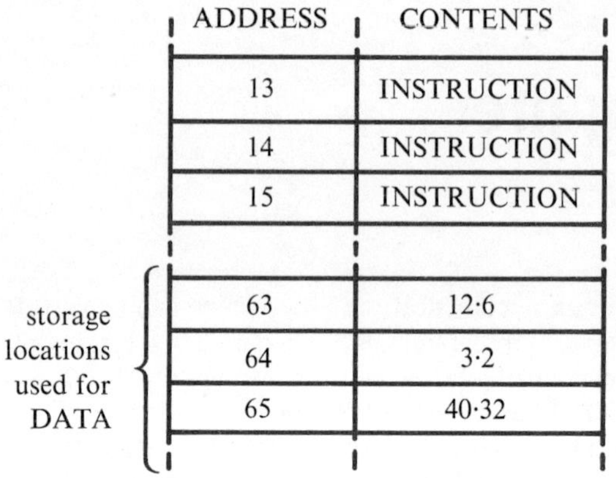

ADDRESS	CONTENTS
13	INSTRUCTION
14	INSTRUCTION
15	INSTRUCTION
63	12·6
64	3·2
65	40·32

storage locations used for DATA

Diagram representing the store of a simple computer

fig. 1

We shall also assume that each storage location of the computer store can hold either an integer or a decimal fraction, and that there is no need to differentiate between these two types of number. Finally, we assume that it is not necessary to express numbers in binary form before entering them into the computer, even though the internal storage and arithmetic of a real machine would be in binary. In most computers, the translation from decimal to binary is performed by the internal logic of the machine.

2.4 the arithmetic unit

Most mathematical computations involve a large number of basic arithmetic operations on the numbers held in the computer store. These operations are performed by the arithmetic unit which can be thought of as a binary operator on the elements of the set of numbers stored in the computer. In our hypothetical computer, we assume that the arithmetic unit is able to perform the basic operations of adding, subtracting, multiplying and dividing, and also to decide on a course of action if the contents of a particular storage location are greater than or equal to the contents of another storage location. These 'decision elements' will be dealt with more fully in chapter 3.

2.5 a cheap model

After the experience of the computer game, the pupil can gain an insight into the workings of our hypothetical machine by building a 'matchbox computer' (ref. 1). The size of the computer is dependent on the number of matchboxes the pupil is able to collect, but most of the problems and programs in this book can be simulated on this simple device. A set of matchboxes is used to represent the computer store, and the contents of the store are written on small cards held inside the matchboxes. Each box is given an address, which is written on the outside, and two further boxes are labelled Input and Output. Arithmetic operations are performed as required with pencil and paper. The important lessons to be learned are how to prepare a problem for a computer and how to recognise problems that are adaptable to computational methods. Later chapters show how problems arising in elementary mathematics can be programmed for even the simplest computational device.

2.6 the control unit

In the matchbox computer the instructions held in the store have to be read in the correct sequence and the operations carried out by hand. These operations may include the transfer of numbers between the store and the arithmetic unit, reading numbers into the store or writing down the contents of a particular storage location. In a full-scale computer, such functions are performed automatically by the *control unit* of the machine.

2.7 an elementary stored program

Let us follow the action of a simple program stored in locations 14, ... 17. We require to multiply the number 12·6 by 3·2.

ADDRESS	CONTENTS
14	Put 12·6 into location 63
15	Put 3·2 into location 64
16	Multiply a copy of the contents of location 63 by a copy of the contents of location 64 and put the result in location 65
17	Print or display the contents of location 65

Control starts here ⟶ (points to location 14)

fig. 2

Control is first set to follow the instruction held in location 14. This is an instruction to put the number 12·6 into location 63, and is called an input instruction. The number 12·6 might be entered on a keyboard, be read from a punched card, punched paper tape or from magnetic tape. In a matchbox computer, the operator must write down the number 12·6 on a card and place this card in matchbox 63. Having obeyed the instruction held in 14, control

20

passes to location 15 (a further input instruction), and hence step by step to the end of the program. Control follows the instructions in sequence unless a decision element is inserted in the program. If such an element is reached, control will 'branch' to a specified address or continue in sequence depending on the result of the decision element.

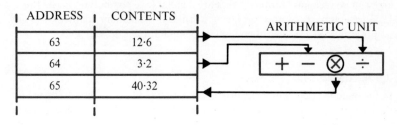

ADDRESS	CONTENTS
63	12·6
64	3·2
65	40·32

fig. 3

The instruction held in location 16 is rather more sophisticated and its action may be illustrated as in fig. 3. Control sends copies of the numbers from the two specified storage locations to the arithmetic unit, instructs the arithmetic unit to multiply and then writes the result in the third specified location. Fig. 3 shows the contents of locations 63, 64 and 65 after the instruction held in location 16 has been carried out. It should be noticed that locations 63 and 64 still contain their original contents.

2.8 the accumulator

Some simple computers are not able to follow this type of instruction, and more programming steps are required. Such computers usually have a location in the arithmetic unit called an *accumulator*, to which we shall give the address A. Numbers are fetched from the store to the accumulator before an arithmetic operation can be performed. If this is the case, then the instruction at address 16 would have to be split into three separate programming steps:

16a	Copy the contents of location 63 into A
16b	Multiply the contents of A by a copy of the contents of location 64 (the result will be held in the accumulator)
16c	Copy the contents of A into location 65

Finally, the instruction held at address 17 (see fig. 2) causes the machine to 'output' the result, 40·32, which has been held in location 65.

2.9 flow charts and programming languages

We have already seen in chapter 1 how a flow chart can be drawn for a particular calculation, and it is convenient if we use symbols in our flow chart which are similar to those in which we write instructions for our computer. Early computers could only accept instructions written in binary code – i.e. a series of 0s and 1s – and the preparation of a program was a long and tedious process. Although this code, known as a *machine code*, is still used to perform the basic operations inside the computer, the labour of preparing the machine code is now performed by a program called a *compiler*. Programming languages have been developed for many different purposes, for example Algol and Fortran (ref. 2) for mathematical and scientific work, and Cobol for use in the business world. These languages use mathematical symbols, decimal digits and letters of the alphabet, and their construction and grammar follow closely the language of mathematics. It is the job of the compiler program to translate these languages into the machine code of a particular computer. Some computers are provided with more than one compiler program, so that different programming languages may be used with a single machine. It is impossible to predict what sort of compiling facilities will be available to the reader on a particular machine, and so the programs and flow charts that follow have been written in a basic language which can be simply adapted to that of any given computer.

2.10 a basic language

The instructions in our program will use algebraic symbols, the arithmetic operators:

$$+ \quad - \quad \times \quad \div,$$

and the relational operators:

$$> \quad = \quad <$$

Readers will find that this language corresponds very closely with that used in the *School Mathematics Project*, A-Level course (ref. 3), and an introduction to such a language may be found in the elementary course books (ref. 4).

Fig. 4 shows how the instructions in fig. 2 can be abbreviated by using these symbols, and fig. 5 shows these instructions in flow-chart form.

We shall expect our machine to understand the words 'input' and 'output', but we shall not worry about the way in which the machine carries out these instructions. How control is made to start at address 14, and finish at 17 will also depend on the particular machine in use, but in the flow charts, these functions will be indicated by the words Begin and End.

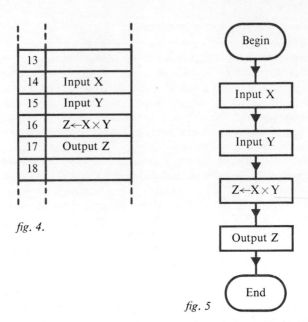

fig. 4.

fig. 5

It is worth stressing at this stage that the symbolic abbreviation for the instruction held in location 16:

$Z \leftarrow X \times Y$

represents a binary operation on the *contents* of the storage locations whose addresses are represented by the symbols X and Y. The result of this operation is then placed in the storage location whose *address* is represented by the symbol Z. By this means we are able to free ourselves from the necessity of allocating numerical addresses to any particular location, this allocation being left to the compiler.

A notation that is often used for representing the *contents* of an address is ( ). For example, in fig. 3, we may write:

$(63) = 12 \cdot 6$ $(64) = 3 \cdot 2,$

and the instruction:

$Z \leftarrow X \times Y,$

may be written:

$(65) \leftarrow (63) \times (64).$

In practice, however, once the difference between the left-hand and right-hand sides of such an instruction is recognised, the pupil will have no difficulty in using the full symbolic form. These instructions are called three-address instructions, and in the flow charts that follow, the computer will be assumed capable of accepting these instructions without any reference to a machine code or even to an accumulator. A summary of the basic language is given below.

INSTRUCTION	EFFECT
A←0 * A←B ** A←−A ***	Set storage location A to zero Copy the contents of location B into location A Change the sign of the contents of location A
Input A Output A	Enter a number into location A from the input device Print or display the contents of location A
A←B+C A←B−C A←B×C A×B÷C	Three address instructions combining copies of the contents of locations B and C and assigning the result to location A

* Equivalent to the three-address instruction $A \leftarrow A - A$
** Equivalent to the three-address instructions

$A \leftarrow A - A$ (clearing store A)
$A \leftarrow A + B$ (i.e. $A \leftarrow 0 + B$)

*** Equivalent to the three-address instructions

$B \leftarrow B - B$ (clearing store B)
$A \leftarrow B - A$ (i.e. $A \leftarrow 0 - A$)

decision elements

The following questions may be used in a flow chart to control the sequence of instructions:

$A > B$? $A = B$? $A < B$?

example Calculate the value of $x^2 + y^2$ for any given value of x and y. Use locations X and Y to hold the initial values of x and y.
Using three-address instructions, the flow chart and program are given in figs. 6 and 7.

In fig. 7, addresses 00, 01, ... 06 have been used for the program.
Addresses 12 and 13 have been used for the values of X and Y. Note that only two data stores are required. For example, the instruction:

$X \leftarrow X \times X$,

replaces the number in location 12 by its square. There is no longer any need to retain the original value of x, and by this means, storage (an expensive item in computers) is saved. The program must occupy consecutive stores, but the choice of addresses for the program and data is arbitrary.

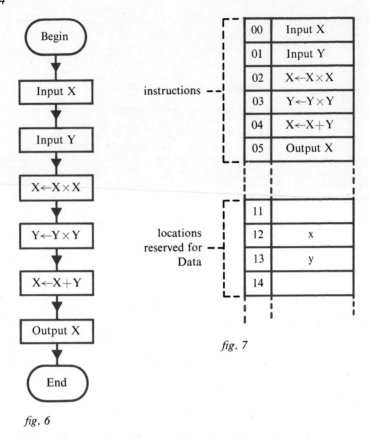

fig. 6

fig. 7

2.11 dry running of programs

Before a simple program is run on a computer, it should be fully tested by hand using trial data. More complex programs should be tested in stages and the final program built up step by step. This process, known as a 'dry run', can be carried out at the flow-chart stage so that logical errors are discovered before computer time is wasted. A slide rule or desk calculating machine can be used to simulate the action of the arithmetic unit, and a table should be made out showing the contents of the data locations at any stage of the computation. For example, if the initial values of X and Y are given as 3·6 and 2·4, the table of values for the program in fig. 7 would be as in the following table.

Program step	Contents of locations	
	12 (i.e. 'X')	13 (i.e. 'Y')
1	3·6	*
2	3·6	2·4
3	12·96	2·4
4	12·96	5·76
5	18·72	5·76

Note that location 13 may initially contain a number from a previous calculation (indicated in the table by *), but in this case it is not necessary to clear
any storage locations before the program is run.

Zero and negative values should be given to the variables to see if this affects
the logic of the computation. Division by zero must be avoided, and such a
mistake can be detected at this stage. Large test values should be tried to see
if the capacity of the machine is likely to be exceeded. Values too great for the
computer will cause an 'overflow', and special programming techniques must
be used when dealing with such values.

When a dry run has been satisfactorily completed, the flow chart can be
translated into a programming language and tested on a computer. If the
results do not agree with the expected answers, either the translation is
incorrect, or the method is unreliable due to errors arising during the computation. Chapter 4 is concerned with such errors and suggests ways of im-
proving programs which have these faults. The correction of the translation
is known as 'de-bugging', and even the most carefully checked program
can show errors at this stage. The pupil will gain a great deal of satisfaction
when his program at last runs successfully, and this will amply repay the time
and trouble spent on the early stages.

2.12 basic algebra and flow charts

The successful construction of flow charts and programs depends on a clear
understanding of the priority of arithmetic operators in algebraic expressions.
The use of a computer with young pupils stimulates interest in the com-
mutative, associative and distributive laws of algebra. For example, the
importance of the associative law becomes clear if flow diagrams are drawn
to calculate $(a \div b) \div c$ and $a \div (b \div c)$. Our simple computer can perform only
one operation at a time, and so the order in which these operations are carried
out is of great importance. The action of the arithmetic unit may be illustrated
as follows:

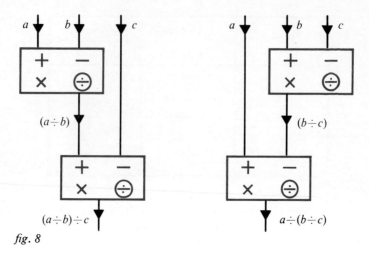

fig. 8

If locations A, B and C initially hold the values of *a*, *b* and *c*, then the corresponding flow charts for generating $(a \div b) \div c$ and $a \div (b \div c)$ are given in fig. 9.

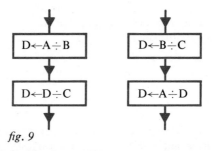

fig. 9

The pupil quickly recognises the difference in the results of such operations, and is able to build up experience which will help him understand more clearly his work with abstract algebraic symbols. The computer enables him to experiment with algebraic constructions, and to test out these constructions with actual data.

The beginner should make himself thoroughly familiar with the techniques of basic programming. A good exercise is to draw flow charts for the construction of elementary functions using the minimum of instructions and storage. In practice, it is not necessary to employ such 'elegance', but it is an enjoyable mathematical exercise and a good programming discipline. The following example is one of many that can be drawn from the work normally covered in the lower school.

example If storage locations A, B and C initially contain the values of the radius of a cylinder, *r*, its length, *h*, and the constant 3·142, draw flow charts to calculate the volume and surface area of the cylinder.

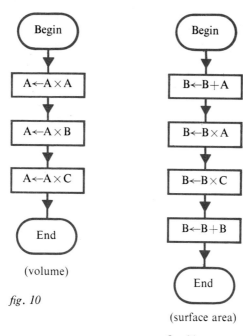

(volume)

fig. 10

(surface area)

fig. 11

The following table shows the initial and final contents of locations A, B and C:

	fig. 10			fig. 11		
	A	B	C	A	B	C
initial	r	h	3·142	r	h	3·142
final	$\pi r^2 h$	h	3·142	r	$2\pi r(h+r)$	3·142

It should be noticed how storage requirements are kept to a minimum by the constant re-use of individual locations.

Once the program for a basic algebraic formula has been constructed, the pupil should have a clear idea of the importance of the various components of the formula. For example, the formula $V = \pi r^2 h$ for calculating the volume of a circular cylinder (fig. 10) can be constructed in different ways depending on the information given. If h and π are known constants, then the construction is:

$$r \to r^2 \to r^2 h \to \pi r^2 h, \tag{1}$$

whereas if r and π are constants, the construction is:

$$h \to rh \to r^2 h \to \pi r^2 h. \tag{2}$$

The computer may now be used as a programmed calculating machine to investigate the effect on the formula if the components are changed in value. Program (1) calculates the volume given the radius, r, and program (2) calculates the volume given the length, h.

Using these programs, the two constructions should be tested with several different values of r and h, and graphs should be plotted of the resulting values of V. The various curves (fig. 12) give insight into the relative importance of the algebraic symbols.

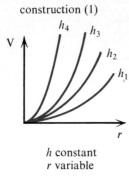

construction (1)   construction (2)

h constant r constant
r variable h variable

fig. 12

Work of this kind is very valuable when discussing the basic ideas of proportionality in formulae such as:

$$V \propto r^2 \quad \text{and} \quad V \propto h.$$

2.13 the computer in the science laboratory

Wherever possible, the work of 2.12 should be accompanied by, and arise out of, suitable experiments in the science laboratory. If several pupils are measuring the volumes of cylinders of different heights or radii, the computer can be used to help plot graphs of the results of experiments as they are being performed. In this way, experimental values that differ from the normal by a large amount can be quickly detected and such experiments can be repeated at once. Often the impact of such work is lost through the time delay between experiment and data analysis.

Alternatively, using the methods outlined in chapter 3, the average of a set of experimental data can be quickly found at the end of a practical period. For example, a rearrangement of the formula $V = \pi r^2 h$ in the form:

$$\pi = \frac{V}{r^2 h}$$

gives a possible way of finding a value of the constant π. A cylindrical container can be filled with known quantities of water and the depth of the water, h, can be determined by direct measurement. The computer can be used to calculate the value of V/r^2h for a large number of different measurements of V, r and h. The results of many experiments can then be averaged to find a reliable class estimate for the constant π.

2.14 nested multiplication (This section may be omitted at a first reading.)

When investigating the solution of quadratic, cubic or higher order equations. it is often necessary to evaluate polynomial functions such as

$$f : x \rightarrow 2x^3 + 2x^2 + 4x + 7$$

Each term could be evaluated and stored separately before accumulating a final total. This method would require three multiplications to obtain $2x^3$, two for $2x^2$, one for $4x$ and three additions, i.e. a total of nine operations to evaluate the polynomial for any given value of x. A more satisfactory method for computing work is described below.

Pupils can be encouraged to construct their own polynomials in the following way:

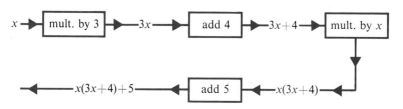

The output is the mapping:

$$x \rightarrow 3x^2 + 4x + 5.$$

It will be noticed that the *numbers* in the operation boxes are the coefficients of the polynomial:

$$3x^2 + 4x + 5,$$

and that they appear in the same order as in the function. This method is known as 'nested multiplication', and the above function can be written in the form:

$$(3x + 4)x + 5.$$

In a similar way, our original function:

$$f : x \rightarrow 2x^3 + 2x^2 + 4x + 7,$$

can be written as:

$$((2x + 2)x + 4)x + 7.$$

If storage locations A, B, C and D hold the values of the coefficients 2, 2, 4 and 7, the flow chart in fig. 13 can be used to evaluate the polynomial for different values of x. The computer can thus be used to help plot a graph showing the 'shape' of the function and the graph can lead to a discussion of interesting features of the polynomial – for example, those values of x which make the function zero.

Work of this kind leads naturally to methods for finding the roots of polynomial equations, and some of these methods are discussed in chapter 7.

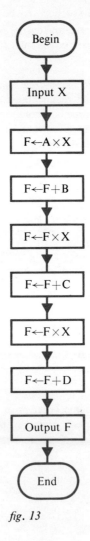

fig. 13

3 elements of programming

3.1 introduction

We now consider some of the difficulties which need to be anticipated when writing a program and some of the programming techniques used to overcome such difficulties. The best way to teach programming techniques is for the teacher, together with the class, to tackle the task of writing a flow chart to solve a particular problem. The flow chart can then be adapted and improved as suggestions are made. Consider the problem of calculating a batsman's average at cricket, according to the formula:

$$a = \frac{r}{b-n},$$

where a is his average, r the total runs scored, b the number of innings and n the number of times not out. Fig. 1 could act as a basis for discussion and adaptation.

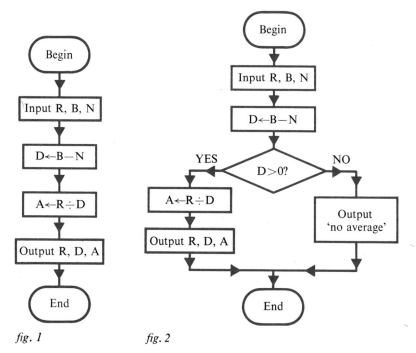

fig. 1   fig. 2

3.2 decisions

It should not be too difficult for the class to see that if $b-n=0$ the flow chart calls for division by zero. In fact it is usual practice to insist that a batsman should have been 'out' at least once before an average is calculated for him. We should now like our flow chart to include an inspection of the input data and then to allow for two alternative courses of action.

Essentially, the computer will have to make a decision. Thus the class is introduced to a decision element and the amended flow chart might be as in fig. 2.

Even the simplest languages used on computers include decision elements with two possible answers to the question asked: YES or NO. Some high-level languages allow for three exits from a decision box or even more in some instances.

3.3 loops

A program to calculate the batting averages for all the members of a team would lead naturally to the use of a loop, which is a technique employed to

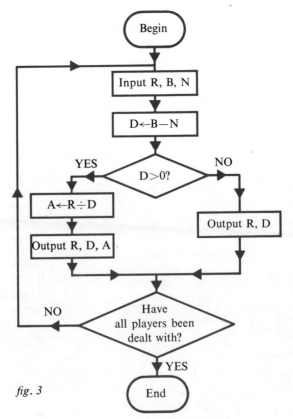

fig. 3

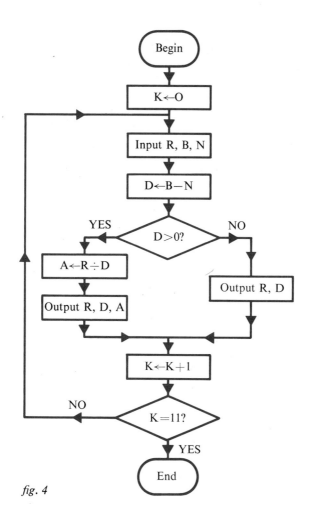

fig. 4

make a computer go back and repeat all or part of a program with different data. In figs. 1 and 2, after the instruction Output R, D, A, we want the computer to Input R, B, N if there is another average to be calculated and to End if no more averages are required. The flow chart would be essentially the same as fig. 2 but with the addition shown in fig. 3. The class should realise that the final question in fig. 3 is not in a form in which it could be included in an actual computer program, yet without such a question the computer would have no means of deciding which of the two available branches to follow. If the End instruction were to be removed, the computer would try to go round the loop for ever, failing only when it could not obey the input instruction because of lack of data. We now consider two techniques which deal with this situation.

3.4 counters

A counter is a device for counting the number of times a computer has gone round a loop, i.e. the number of times the same calculations have been repeated. We are thus able to make the computer leave the loop when the counter has reached a certain predetermined value, say 11 in the case of the cricket team. We use a variable k for the counter which is put equal to zero *outside the loop* and is increased by one each time the loop is completed. (The class might consider what happens if the instruction $K \leftarrow 0$ comes inside the loop.) The flow chart is given in fig. 4. In this case we knew the number of players for whom we were calculating an average, but it is conceivable that this information may not be available. We now deal with this situation, and introduce a technique which will make our program more flexible and capable of dealing with any number of players.

3.5 false data

After the final items of data have been fed into the computer, we arrange for 'false' data to follow. In our cricket example, $r = 100\,000$, $b = 1$, $n = 1$ would do.

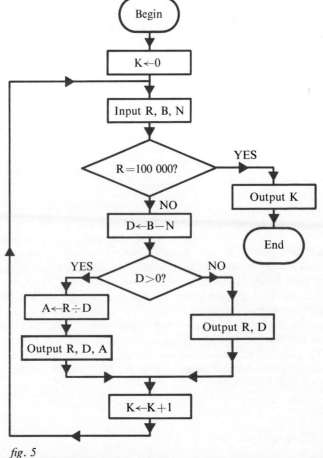

fig. 5

These false items of data must be unlikely to arise in the ordinary course of events. We insert into the program a question to see whether this number has been read or not. If this number has been read, we require the program to 'jump' to End – if not, the program must continue as before. An ordinary decision element will do very well.

We could retain our counter so that at the end of the program the computer could tell us how many averages had been calculated. Fig. 5 shows the final flow chart.

Turning our attention away from cricket, a program to calculate values of x^n for a given value of x and successive values of n from 1 to 10 would make use of a loop and a counter. The flow chart is given in fig. 6. The class should note the instruction $Z \leftarrow Z \times X$ which uses the value of, say, x^3 to calculate the value of x^4, etc. and 'overwrites' the previous contents of location Z each time.

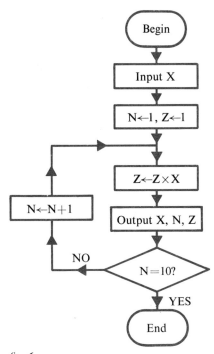

fig. 6

36

3.6 nested loops

If the flow chart in fig. 6 is adapted to cope with values of x from 1 to 10 in steps of 1 we shall be using two loops in one program. It is important when this happens (and when more than two loops are used) that the loops should be 'nested', i.e. if the two loops are not completely separate then one must lie completely inside the other. In diagrammatic form the arrangements in fig. 7a are permissible and those in fig. 7b are not.

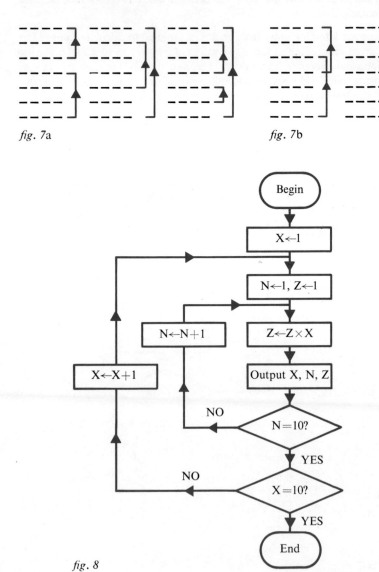

fig. 7a   fig. 7b

fig. 8

The flow chart for the adapted program is given in fig. 8. The teacher should emphasise the fact that the larger loop jumps back to $N \leftarrow 1$, $Z \leftarrow 1$. When the program has output a set of powers of one value of x, n and z must be put equal to 1 again before the powers of the next value of x are calculated. Points such as this are a common cause of error when pupils are writing their own programs.

examples A

1 Write a flow chart to calculate the area of a circle, given the radius. Output the radius and area.

2 Write a flow chart to calculate the volume of a right circular cylinder, given the base radius and the height. Output the radius, height and volume.

3 Write a flow chart to calculate the surface area and volume of a sphere of given radius. Use the value of the surface area to help you calculate the volume, and output the radius, area and volume.

4 Adapt the flow chart in question 1 to calculate the area as the radius goes from 1 cm to 10 cm in steps of 1 cm. Output the radius and area each time.

5 Write a flow chart to calculate the volumes of right circular cylinders having the same base radius but heights of 1, 2, 4, 8, 16, 32 cm. Output the radius, height and volume each time. What do you notice about your results?

6 Write a flow chart to calculate the volumes of right circular cylinders having the same height but base radii of 1, 2, 4, 8, 16, 32 cm. Output the height, radius and volume each time. What do you notice about your results?

7 Write a flow chart to calculate the square and cube of a given number. Hence write a program to calculate the squares and cubes of the integers from 1 to 30. Each time output the number, its square and its cube.

8 For unequal values of b and c, the values of $x=b^2-c^2$, $y=2bc$ and $z=b^2+c^2$ give possible sides of a right-angled triangle. Write a flow chart to output Pythagorean triples, for integral values of b and c less than 9.

9 The formula $\dfrac{P \times R \times T}{100}$ gives the simple interest £I on a sum of money £P invested for T years at R per cent per year. Write a flow chart to calculate the interest for a given sum of money, rate and time. This flow chart may be adapted in several ways: by taking the rate from 0 to 5 per cent in steps of $\frac{1}{4}$, keeping the time and the sum of money constant; by varying the time; by varying the sum of money (often called the principal). You may even care to make your own simple interest tables.

10   The 'radian' is a unit of angular measure; one radian is the angle subtended at the centre of a circle by an arc length equal to the radius of the circle. If d is the number of degrees in a given angle and r is the number of radians in the same angle, they are connected by the formula:

$$r = \frac{\pi d}{180}.$$

Write flow charts to convert an angle from degrees to radians and vice versa.

3.7 ordering data

In our basic language we have permitted ourselves the questions $A = B$? and $A > B$? The second question is equivalent to asking $B < A$? if this is required in a program. A simpler basic language may have only the question $A > 0$? and to ask $B > C$? we should first have to write $D \leftarrow B - C$ and then ask $D > 0$? Some languages provide for three exits from a decision element according as $A < 0$, $A = 0$, $A > 0$. One important use of decisions in a program is to arrange a set of numbers in ascending or descending order.

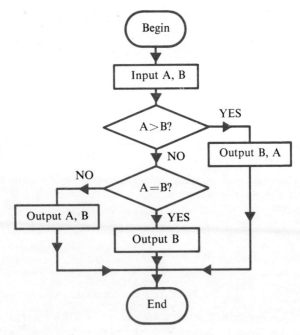

fig. 9

The class may well suggest, while working on the cricket averages above, that it would be desirable to arrange them in order of merit. It is not a simple task to program a computer to do this, but in fig. 9 we show how two numbers may be arranged in ascending order. This flow chart deals with numbers which are positive or negative or fractional. A similar flow chart to output three numbers, A, B, C in descending order is correspondingly longer, and can be based on a similar method. If a large number of numbers is to be sorted, then the above method becomes unwieldy and must be adapted. This can be done by introducing the concept of a 'subroutine'.

3.8 subroutines

Simple computers can carry out the operations of addition, subtraction, multiplication and division, and simple branch instructions. If, in a given calculation, a square root is required, then its value must either be obtained from a set of tables and entered as data or be calculated by a special set of instructions. This set is called a 'subroutine' and can be called for whenever a square root is required. In large computers, several standard subroutines are available and may be called for using instructions such as:

$$X \leftarrow LOG(Y); \quad X \leftarrow TAN(Y).$$

These built-in functions cover a wide range and depend on the type of computer being used. Some computers can accept a single instruction of the form:

$$X \leftarrow SIN(\sqrt{(1+X^2)}),$$

and call the appropriate subroutines automatically.

Suppose that in the course of a program the formula $s = ut + \frac{1}{2}at^2$ is used several times for different values of t. This could be done by means of a loop. An alternative method is to place in the computer store a program to calculate s from this formula, and to give it a name to which we may refer in our program. The name may be for example DIST (T) in exactly the same way as we might refer to LOG (X). If, in our main program, we require the value of s when $t = 2.4$, we simply use the instruction S ← DIST (2.4). The computer immediately jumps out of our program to the subroutine program, does the calculation, and then jumps back to the main program. The subroutine program need not necessarily be a calculation from a formula: it could be any sequence of instructions that can be obeyed by the computer.

3.9 the swop sort

To return to our problem of arranging a set of numbers in descending order, we look at a 'sorting routine' program. Let us call it the 'swop sort' program.

	A	B	C	D
	4	6	9	3
Inspect A, B – swop				
	6	4	9	3
Inspect B, C – swop				
	6	9	4	3
Inspect C, D – leave				
	6	9	4	3
	2 swops			
Inspect A, B – swop				
	9	6	4	3
Inspect B, C – leave				
	9	6	4	3
Inspect C, D – leave				
	9	6	4	3
	1 swop			
Inspect A, B – leave				
	9	6	4	3
Inspect B, C – leave				
	9	6	4	3
Inspect C, D – leave				
	9	6	4	3
	0 swops			
End				

fig. 10

Given a set of numbers in locations A, B, C, D, etc., our program inspects the numbers in A and B and rearranges them if necessary so that the larger is in A and the smaller is in B. If the two numbers are equal we leave them alone. The number now in B is compared with the number in C and they are rearranged if necessary. The new C is compared with D, and so on. At the same time we count up the number of times a swop is actually made until we come to the end of the list. The new list is scanned again from the beginning and the number of swops made is again counted. This process is repeated until the number of swops in a complete scan is zero. The numbers will then be in descending order in locations A, B, C, D, etc. Fig. 10 shows an example involving four locations. The contents of these locations at each stage of the program are given until a scan of three inspections yields no swops.

Fig. 11 shows the flow chart for a subroutine called SWOP (X, Y) which arranges the numbers in X and Y as required. Note that if a swop has been made, k will have the value 1 at the end of the subroutine; if no swop has been made, k will have the value 0.

A flow chart making use of this subroutine to sort four numbers in locations A, B, C, D, is given in fig. 12. Note that each time the subroutine has been used, the instruction $I \leftarrow I+K$ increases i by 1 if a swop has been made, and increases i by 0 if no swop has been made.

The speed of this process can be improved if we notice that after one complete scan, location D holds the smallest of the four numbers. This location may be omitted from the next scan. Similarly location C may be omitted after the second scan is complete, and so on until no further swops are required.

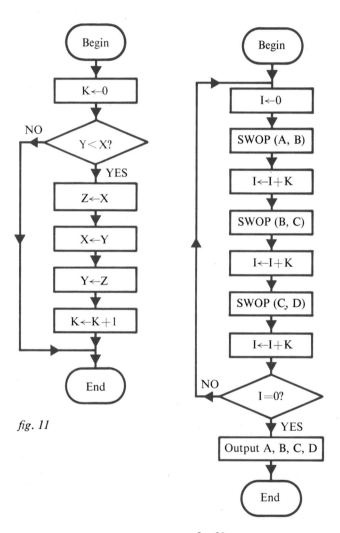

fig. 11

fig. 12

3.10 the search routine

This is a more difficult topic – not recommended for the less able pupil. The swop-sort program gradually sorts the list of numbers into order. An alternative method is to look for the biggest number in the list – such a method is called a 'search routine'. We would use this method if we were interested only in the largest number of a list.

In the following example we shall assume that all the numbers are positive, and that we know how many there are – say twenty.

Suppose that the numbers are in the storage locations A_1, A_2, ... A_{20}. We first put the number in A_1 into a location called MAX. We now compare the numbers in MAX and A_2 and put the larger in location MAX (which may well mean that the number in MAX remains the same).

This is continued until MAX has been compared with A_{20}. Each time a number is put into MAX we keep a note of its original address in a location J, say. At the end of the process, MAX contains the largest of the twenty numbers. To find the second largest number we really want the largest number removed from the set of twenty. It is easier, however, to replace the largest number by a number which we know is less than any of the original twenty numbers (for example a negative number). This is done so that we still have twenty addresses and our program need not be altered (changing the program to consider nineteen addresses, then eighteen addresses, etc., would be too complicated). The whole process is now repeated, the number in MAX at the end being the second largest number of the original twenty. We can now output MAX and change the contents of the appropriate location to another negative number. We continue in this way until all the twenty numbers have been placed in order.

Fig. 13 shows the flow chart for the search routine. The following points should be noted.

(1) The counter N ensures that the program stops after having found MAX for the twentieth time.
(2) The variable J records the location of the number currently in MAX.
(3) The counter I ensures that we compare MAX with successive numbers in the list, and that the computer does not look for more than twenty numbers. Using A_I as I takes successive integral values is known as using a 'subscripted variable'.
(4) The instruction $A_J = -J$ is a neat method for putting unequal negative numbers into those locations whose numbers have been displayed in MAX.

If our original twenty numbers were to contain some negative numbers, the flow chart could easily be adapted to cover this case. We simply replace the instruction $A_J = -J$ by an instruction such as $A_J = J - 10\ 000$, which ensures numbers smaller than any in the original list.

The program will delete only one number on each loop and if there are any equal numbers in the original list, MAX will be the same on successive outputs. If we do not know how many numbers there are originally, the technique of false data can be applied as described above. The reader may care to adapt the flow chart in fig. 13, making use of a subroutine.

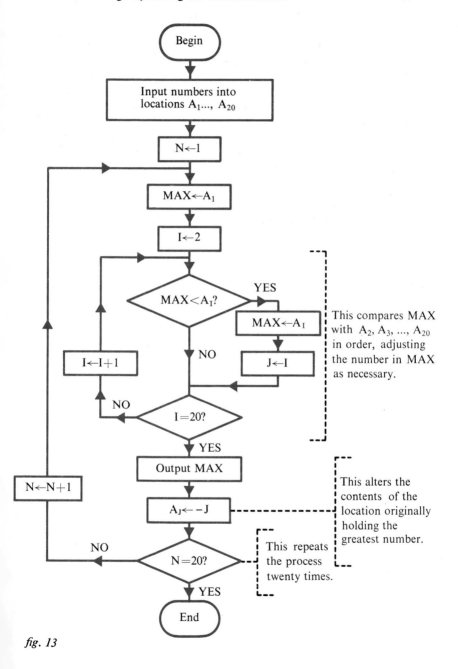

fig. 13

3.11 data processing

The last two programs have shown the computer in a rather different light. So far we have covered only numerical calculations, but now we have shown that the computer is able to sort data. In fact data processing accounts for more programs in modern computer usage than do numerical calculations.

In fig. 14 we show a flow chart to input the ages of all the pupils in a school and to output the numbers in the age groups 11–14 inclusive, 15–16 inclusive and 17 or over. We assume that there are no pupils under the age of 11, but the reader may care to make the necessary additions to the flow chart to cover the case where such pupils belong to the school. The ages are taken to be recorded in the form 16·01 for 16 years 1 month, etc. up to 16·11 for 16 years 11 months. A false age of 100 is used for the last piece of data.

It is left as an exercise for the reader to adapt the flow chart to output the percentages of pupils in the various age groups.

The teacher will find that classes enjoy examples such as this one and the school administration should provide many ideas for programs.

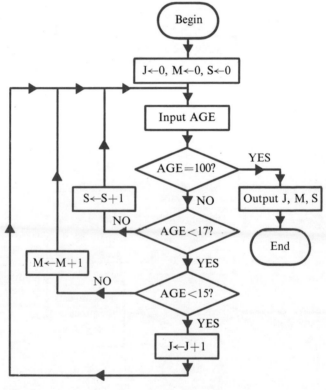

fig. 14

3.12 matrices

Matrices, as stores of information, have already been mentioned in chapter 1. Programs to manipulate matrices require the use of double subscripts such as A_{12}, A_{13}, etc. These techniques are dealt with fully in most programming manuals (refs. 1, 2, 3, 4). We shall restrict ourselves to row and column matrices and single subscripts. Fig. 15 gives a flow chart for multiplying together the row matrix $(A_0A_1A_2A_3)$ and the column matrix

$$\begin{pmatrix} B_0 \\ B_1 \\ B_2 \\ B_3 \end{pmatrix}$$

Notice how the loop also includes the input of the matrices.

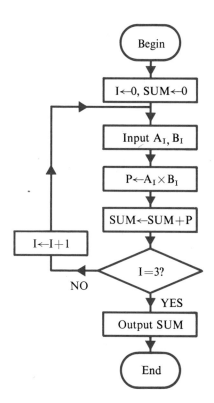

fig. 15

3.13 non-numerical situations

We now use our computer to arrange a set of names in alphabetical order. Pupils may have the idea that a computer can deal only with numbers. It should be pointed out to them that the computer does not deal with numbers but with the coded representations of numbers. All we have to do is to replace our letters with a number code and the computer can deal with words. Large computers have a simple method of making this translation, but we shall have to do our own coding and decoding into numbers and back to letters.

A good introduction might be to give some members of the class a well-shuffled pack of cards each and ask them to arrange the pack into the order A, 2, 3, 4, ... J, Q, K in each of the suits in the order Clubs, Diamonds, Hearts, Spades. It is possible that someone may look for the Ace of Clubs, then the two of Clubs, then the three of Clubs, etc., but it is most unlikely. They will probably adopt some system that involves a preliminary sorting into, say, black and red suits, then into separate suits, then each suit might be arranged in order and finally the four suits put together in the order required. A similar method can be used for alphabetical sorting.

Represent each letter by a two-digit code: 01 for A, 02 for B, etc. and 26 for Z. The name GREEN would thus be represented by the number 0718050514. The numerical equivalents of the names can be fed into the computer and can then be sorted by either of the methods mentioned above. However, a swop sort of such numbers would present a few difficulties, not the least being the size of the numbers involved: a name of eight letters will require sixteen digits. It would save a considerable amount of computer time if the sort were to proceed along the lines of the card-sorting above. For example, the first pair of digits of each name could be inspected, and the numbers arranged in order accordingly. There would be a block of numbers starting with 01 ..., then a block starting 02 ..., etc. Next we would take all the numbers starting 01 ..., inspect the second pair of digits and subdivide this first block into smaller blocks. Then, if necessary, the third pair of digits could be inspected and so on until the sort is complete. The program would probably involve several subroutines and would be far from brief. The reader may care to try a simple case for himself.

3.14 games playing

A section on the non-numerical applications of the computer would not be complete without at least some reference to the games-playing abilities of the computer, or rather the ability of man to program games for the computer. Games such as Noughts and Crosses, Nim, Draughts and Chess have all been investigated with greater or lesser success.

The programming of Noughts and Crosses was the first problem to be tackled and solved. There are nine squares, but because of the symmetry of the figure there are only three distinct opening moves, and further moves are also

47

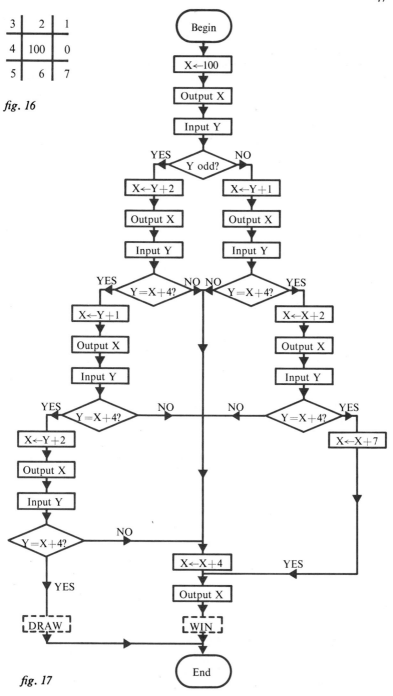

3	2	1
4	100	0
5	6	7

fig. 16

fig. 17

simplified. In the flow chart of fig. 17 the nine squares are identified by the numbers in fig. 16. All the arithmetic in the flow chart is in modulo 8. The instructions are in terms of X and Y rather than X and 0, the instruction X←4 meaning Put an X in square 4; the instruction Y←X+6 following this would mean Put a 0 in square 2. The computer has to have some way of knowing where its opponent has placed his last 0, hence the instruction Input Y in which the number of the square last occupied by the opponent has to be fed into the computer.

The flow chart is not an exhaustive treatment of every possible game of Noughts and Crosses, being concerned only with the situation where the computer has the first move and occupies the centre square. However, the game that starts in this way is carried to its logical conclusion; it is simplified to the extent that each computer-move may have equivalent symmetrical moves which would be just as effective and would give the computer's game some variety. Other analyses are left as exercises for the reader.

Nim (ref. 5) is well suited to the computer, being based on the binary system, and is similar to Noughts and Crosses in that the first player, if he plays correctly, cannot lose.

Chess and Draughts are games of far greater complexity, and much work is still being done on the programming of them. It is beyond the scope of this book to tackle such a problem, but it may be of interest to indicate the approach. The program would have to indicate legal moves and have a method of storing the progress of the game. In addition, the program would have to evaluate the strength of any piece according to its position on the board and its position relative to the other pieces. If the computer were to consider all possible moves in a game, even the most modern computer would not finish the game before its opponent died of old age.

The most modern approach (involving highly sophisticated techniques) is to get the computer to learn from its own experience in playing the game and thus adapt its future play.

examples B

1   Write a flow chart to input four unequal numbers, placing the largest in location L and the smallest in location S.

2   Write a flow chart to input a set of three numbers and to test whether or not they could be the lengths of the sides of a triangle. If they can be the sides of a triangle, test whether the triangle is obtuse-angled, right-angled or acute-angled.

3   Extend the flow chart for question 2 to calculate the area of the triangle.

4   Write a flow chart to input the elements of a 2×2 matrix and then to calculate the inverse matrix. (This, and other examples on matrices, are good tests as to whether the pupil can control the computer output to give a well presented and easily read result.)

5 Write a flow chart to input the marks gained by the members of your form in their last mathematics exam and to output them in order of merit. This may be adapted to calculate the percentage mark and if it is below a certain level chosen by you, to print out the mark accompanied by the word 'Fail'; if it is above the chosen level to print out the mark accompanied by the word 'Pass'.

6 Use a swop-sort method to arrange the following names in alphabetical order: Alf, Joe, Bill, Fred, John.

7 Write a flow chart to input a man's salary, his income tax code number, his superannuation rate and any other relevant details, and to output his gross pay, his income tax, his superannuation, his national insurance and his net pay.

8 Write a flow chart to input four number pairs representing towns, and to calculate the distance travelled (as the crow flies) by all possible routes which connect the four towns. Hence find the shortest possible route which takes in the four towns.

4 errors

4.1 slide-rule accuracy

Using a pencil and paper, a pupil can accurately perform the multiplication:

$$43{\cdot}8 \times 2{\cdot}77 = 121{\cdot}326.$$

If, however, a slide rule is used to work out this product, the following difficulties are encountered.

(1) The original data (i.e. the numbers 43·8 and 2·77) cannot be set on the scales of the rule exactly. On a 10-inch rule, the position of the digit 8 has to be judged between the marked divisions of 43·5 and 44·0 (see fig. 1),

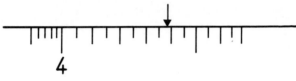

fig. 1

and the position of 2·77 has to be judged between the marks for 2·76 and 2·78 (see fig. 2).

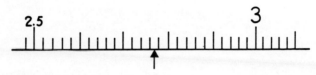

fig. 2

(2) An estimate of the size of the answer has to be made. Working mentally to one significant figure, the estimate is:

$$40 \times 3 = 120 \simeq 100 \text{ (one sig. fig.).}$$

Carelessness in making this approximation can lead to an incorrect positioning of the decimal point in the answer.

(3) Knowing that the answer is in the region of 100, the pupil has then to estimate the answer from the slide-rule scale. He is lucky if he can manage

to read 121·3 with any confidence – his answers are more likely to lie some-where between 121 and 122. Giving the answer to the nearest scale division yields the result 121 – which is correct to three significant figures, but a slight misreading of the scales could easily lead to an answer of 122.

On a 5-inch slide rule, the problem is more acute, and the division nearest to the answer is 122. Most teachers are content to allow a two significant-figure answer for such a rule, and so in this case 120 would be reasonable.

The problem we are meeting in these examples is lack of accuracy in our computing device. No machine can give unlimited accuracy, and an estimate of the errors involved during a computation should accompany a statement of the answer. For example,

by desk calculating machine,

$$43·8 \times 2·77 = 121·326 \text{ (exactly)};$$

by 10-inch slide rule,

$$43·8 \times 2·77 = 121·3 \text{ (last figure estimated)}$$
$$= 121 \quad \text{(three sig. fig.)};$$

by 5-inch slide rule,

$$43·8 \times 2·77 = 121 \text{ (last figure estimated)}$$
$$= 120 \text{ (two sig. fig.)}.$$

4.2 exact calculations on inexact data
If our computing machine is able to work exactly with the input data (as with the desk machine above), there still remains the possibility that the data are only approximate. The product $43·8 \times 2·77$ may have arisen when finding the cost of 43·8 metres of stair carpet at £2·77 per metre. Here, the price £2·77 may be exact, but the length 43·8 metres is only as accurate as the measuring device used when cutting the carpet. Similarly, a computation involving π or the trigonometrical multipliers will have to be performed on inexact data, because of the irrationality of numbers such as sin 45°. (How accurate, even, was the measurement of the angle?)

Most practical computations will therefore include an element of error, and the programmer must make sure that these errors are understood, and are under control. In some circumstances, for example when dealing with money, exact results will be required from exact data. Successful performance of such computations on a machine will depend on the capacity of the machine and on the organisation of the program.

4.3 limitations of storage – floating-point arithmetic
If the individual locations of a computer store are able to hold up to four decimal digits, then without any further information the only numbers that can be stored are the integers from 0 to 9999. To include negative numbers, each

52

location must also hold a positive or negative sign. This may be illustrated by considering each storage location as split into five compartments – one containing the sign, and the remaining four containing the significant digits. Location 63, holding the integer −325 is illustrated in fig. 3.

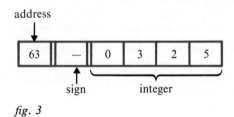

fig. 3

A machine which can work only with integers from −9999 to +9999 is of little use for our purpose, for no work can be done in decimals. This problem can be overcome by a slight increase in storage and by the use of *floating-point arithmetic*. In floating-point arithmetic, all numbers are given to the maximum number of digits that can be held in each location, and the position of the decimal point is fixed by a sign and an index. This representation of numbers is similar to *standard index form*, except that the index is always one greater than the corresponding value in standard index form. For example, the number 23·6 would be expressed as $0·2360 \times 10^2$ and stored as in fig. 4.

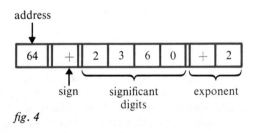

fig. 4

Further examples are given in the following table:

number	standard index form	floating-point form	as stored
0·0001867	$1·867 \times 10^{-4}$	$0·1876 \times 10^{-3}$	$+1876-3$
−7637	$-7·637 \times 10^3$	$-0·7637 \times 10^4$	$-7637+4$
2	2×10^0	$0·2000 \times 10^1$	$+2000+1$

In the discussions that follow, we shall assume that the arithmetic unit of our computer is able to work in floating-point arithmetic, and that all calculations are rounded to the maximum number of digits that can be held by the store.

4.4 truncation and rounding

When correcting a number, say 137·8, to two significant figures, we can either 'truncate' all figures after the second, giving 130, or we can 'round' the number to the *nearest* two-figure approximation (140). Rounding can be illustrated on a number line (fig. 5) by taking the nearest two-figure division as an approximation. Truncating means taking the division just less than the given number.

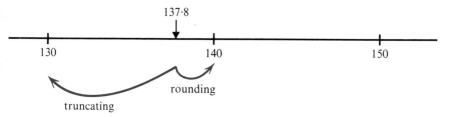

fig. 5

Figs. 6 and 7 show how cases of extreme error can arise. The maximum error in truncating is seen to be one full-scale division, whereas in rounding, the maximum error is only a half-scale division.

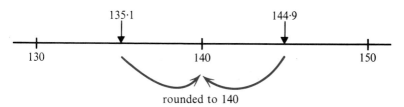

fig. 6

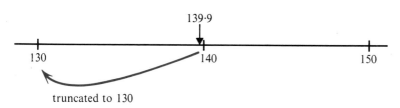

fig. 7

When rounding a number such as 139·5 to three significant figures, a possible ambiguity arises. The rule most generally used is to take 140 as the rounded value (i.e. correct 'up'), but a better rule is to correct always to an *even* last digit so that errors of this type are averaged out, and subsequent division by 2 leads to a whole-number answer.

4.5 mechanisation of the rounding process

Assume that the arithmetic unit of our computer can accept floating-point numbers of up to two digits in length, and that the output number is also rounded to two significant figures. In some ways this is similar to the use of a 5-inch slide rule, and some of the examples that follow can be illustrated to a class on a 5-inch rule. As with the slide rule, the position of the decimal point will be fixed independently. The two-digit arithmetic unit can be imagined to have two input registers, and an accumulator which can hold four digits. After the multiplication has been carried out, the product 34 × 47 will be held as follows:

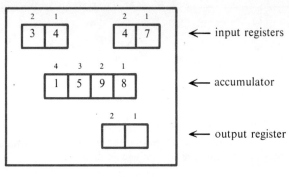

fig. 8

Fig. 8 shows the digits held in the registers before the rounding process, and each digit position in the registers has been given a number. We shall now use the facility of 'left' or 'right shifting' the contents of a register. For example, if the contents of the accumulator are right shifted two places, this register will then show

4	3	2	1
0	0	1	5

thus *truncating* the number 1598 to two significant figures.

If the contents are now transferred to the output register, the result would be read as 1500 (assuming the decimal point has been fixed correctly).

In order to *round* a number in the accumulator to two significant figures, we may proceed as follows.

(1) Left or right shift until three significant figures remain in positions 1, 2 and 3 of the accumulator:

4	3	2	1
0	1	5	9

(2) Add 5 to position 1 of the accumulator:

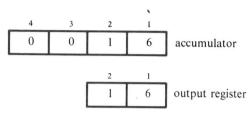

(3) Right shift one place and transfer the result to the output register:

4	3	2	1	
0	0	1	6	accumulator

2	1	
1	6	output register

The result will now be put into store as 1600, showing that the rounding process has been carried out correctly. The reader is encouraged to try other cases for himself, preferably using a desk machine.

4.6 error analysis

The formal study of error analysis uses the terms *absolute* and *relative error*, and we shall define these terms before showing how such ideas can be explained to pupils.

absolute error

If n is an approximation to an exact number N, then the error, e, in the approximation is defined by

$$N = n + e \quad \text{(sometimes as } n = N + e)$$

and the *absolute error* by $|e|$ (i.e. the positive value of e).

relative error

It is important to consider errors in comparison with the size of the approximate number, and so we define *relative error* as the ratio:

$$|e| \, / \, |N|,$$

where e and N are defined as above.

The *percentage relative error* can be calculated from the expression:

$$\frac{|e|}{|N|} \times 100,$$

and this parameter is useful in descriptive work. In practice, however, relative error can be expressed more simply by stating the number of accurate significant figures. In the rounding process, the absolute error is less than or equal to half a unit in the next significant figure. The following table shows examples of approximations and the corresponding absolute and relative errors after rounding.

approximation	number of sig. fig.	absolute error	relative error	percentage relative error (%)
13·6	3	$\leqslant 0·05$	$<0·004$	$< 0·4$
2600	4	$\leqslant 0·5$	$<0·0002$	$< 0·02$
2600	2	$\leqslant 50$	$<0·02$	< 2
0·03	1	$\leqslant 0·005$	$<0·2$	<20

In the table, the number 2600 has been shown as correct to four or two significant figures. This confusion can be avoided if the number is expressed in standard index form, in which case zeros after the last non-zero digit are regarded as significant. Then $2·600 \times 10^3$ shows that four significant figures are correct, but $2·6 \times 10^2$ indicates only two figures.

4.7 error accumulation

Whenever a simple arithmetic operation is performed on approximate data, the error in the answer will depend on two factors: the errors in the original data; and the accuracy to which a machine can process the numbers. We shall show how errors accumulate in each of the basic operations, and also how errors are caused by the limitations of size in a particular machine.

addition

If n_1 and n_2 are approximations to the exact numbers N_1 and N_2, with errors e_1 and e_2, then:

$$N_1 = n_1 + e_1 \quad \text{and} \quad N_2 = n_2 + e_2,$$

and so

$$N_1 + N_2 = (n_1 + n_2) + (e_1 + e_2).$$

The absolute error in the sum is therefore given by $|e_1 + e_2|$. It can be proved that (cf. the triangle law for vectors):

$$|e_1 + e_2| \leqslant |e_1| + |e_2|,$$

and so the maximum absolute error in the sum is less than the sum of the absolute errors in the original approximate numbers. This may be demonstrated by giving simple arithmetic examples.

example 1 Add 31·8 to 2·16, where each number is given to three significant figures.

The numbers will be added as follows:

	absolute error
31·8	⩽0·05
+ 2·16	⩽0·005
33·96	

The error in the answer will be less than or equal to:

0·05+0·005=0·055.

The best estimate for the answer is therefore between:

33·96+0·055   and   33·96−0·055,

i.e. between 34·015 and 33·905. The best answer we can give with certainty is 34, which therefore gives us only two significant figures compared with the three in the given data.

example 2 Add 31·8 to 2·16 where the arithmetic unit is restricted to only three decimal digits.

In example 1, we assumed that it was possible to 'line up' the numbers 31·8 and 2·16 before adding, without loss of digits. However, in a machine of limited size, a further error is introduced during the line-up process.

decimal point

Here the maximum absolute errors will be 0·05 for 31·8 and 0·1 for the number 2·1. This last error is a truncation error due to the right shift during line up. The maximum error in the answer, A, is then 0·05+0·1=0·15 giving a range of:

34·05⩾A⩾33·75.

Here again, the most reliable answer, 34, is correct to two significant figures.

example 3 A geometrical illustration may be helpful when explaining the inequality:

$$|e_1+e_2| \leqslant |e_1|+|e_2|.$$

Diagrams can be drawn showing the error part of any approximation:

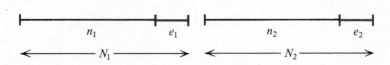

The maximum error in the sum may be illustrated as

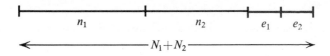

and the case where e_1 and e_2 are of opposite sign:

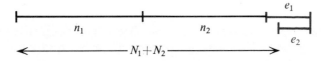

More diagrams are needed for discussion of all possible cases for the signs of e_1 and e_2, but these can be readily drawn.

example 4 Young pupils will probably feel happiest with a purely numerical approach, e.g. Add 2·7 to 3·5 (two sig. fig.).

    2·7 lies between 2·65 and 2·75.
    3·5 lies between 3·45 and 3·55.

Therefore the sum (6·2) lies between 6·10 and 6·30, giving a maximum possible error of 0·1. The most reliable answer is 6 to one significant figure.

subtraction

In the case of subtraction,

$$N_1-N_2=(n_1-n_2)+(e_1-e_2),$$

and again

$$|e_1-e_2| \leqslant |e_1|+|e_2|.$$

The absolute error in a difference is at most the sum of the errors in the original approximations.

This property may again be illustrated as in examples 1–4 above, but the importance of subtraction errors can be seen when dealing with nearly equal numbers. The size of the machine is then of crucial importance.

example 5 On a machine which can give a maximum of four decimal digits, perform the subtraction:

$$3\cdot614 - 3\cdot612,$$

where each number is correct to four significant figures. The answer will be given as:

$0\cdot002000$ (i.e. $0\cdot2000 \times 10^{-2}$ in floating-point form)

but the last three zeros are meaningless. There is no way of achieving greater accuracy than this, and the program must be reorganised to avoid such loss.

multiplication (This section may be omitted at a first reading.)

Using the above notation,

$$N_1N_2 = (n_1 + e_1)(n_2 + e_2)$$
$$= n_1n_2 + n_1e_2 + n_2e_1 + e_1e_2. \tag{1}$$

Because e_1 and e_2 are relatively small, the term e_1e_2 may be neglected, and so the absolute error is:

$$|n_1e_2 + n_2e_1| \leqslant |n_1e_2| + |n_2e_1|. \tag{2}$$

In this case, we get a more simple relationship if we work in terms of relative error. The relative error:

$$= |n_1e_2 + n_2e_1| \ / \ |n_1n_2|$$
$$= \left| \frac{e_1}{n_1} + \frac{e_2}{n_2} \right|$$
$$\leqslant \left| \frac{e_1}{n_1} \right| + \left| \frac{e_2}{n_2} \right|, \tag{3}$$

i.e. the relative error is at most the sum of the relative errors of the original approximations.

example 6 Multiply $2\cdot7$ by $3\cdot5$ (two sig. fig.)

The answer will lie between

$$2\cdot65 \times 3\cdot45 \quad \text{and} \quad 2\cdot75 \times 3\cdot55.$$

By desk machine, working exactly,

$$2\cdot65 \times 3\cdot45 = 9\cdot1425$$
$$2\cdot7 \ \times 3\cdot5 \ = 9\cdot45$$
$$2\cdot75 \times 3\cdot55 = 9\cdot7625$$

showing a maximum error of $0\cdot3125$, occurring when both errors of $0\cdot05$ are positive. This error can be seen – from equation (1) – to have the components:

$$n_1e_2 + n_2e_1 + e_1e_2 = (2\cdot7)(0\cdot05) + (3\cdot5)(0\cdot05) + (0\cdot05)^2$$
$$= 0\cdot135 + 0\cdot175 + 0\cdot0025$$
$$= 0\cdot3125.$$

The maximum relative errors in the measurements of 2·7 and 3·5 are:

$$\left|\frac{\pm 0 \cdot 05}{2 \cdot 7}\right| \simeq 0 \cdot 019 \quad \text{and} \quad \left|\frac{\pm 0 \cdot 05}{3 \cdot 5}\right| \simeq 0 \cdot 014,$$

respectively. The maximum relative error in the product is given by:

$$\left|\frac{+0 \cdot 3125}{9 \cdot 45}\right| \simeq 0 \cdot 033,$$

showing that equation (3) is satisfied.

Diagrams are helpful to demonstrate the errors accumulated during multiplication. Fig. 9 shows the case where both e_1 and e_2 are positive.

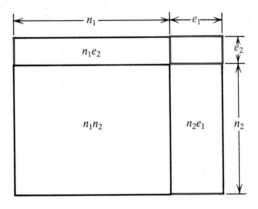

fig. 9

Fig. 9 is especially useful when explaining how e_1e_2 is small compared with n_1e_2 and n_2e_1. If the pupil has not met with the algebraic expansion of $(n_1+e_1)(n_2+e_2)$, then an arithmetic demonstration should suffice.

division (This section may be omitted at a first reading.)

The theory is more difficult in the case of division, because the binomial theorem has to be used to simplify the result:

$$\frac{N_1}{N_2} = \frac{n_1+e_1}{n_2+e_2} = (n_1+e_1)\frac{1}{n_2}\left(1+\frac{e_2}{n_2}\right)^{-1}$$

$$\simeq (n_1+e_1)\frac{1}{n_2}\left(1-\frac{e_2}{n_2}\right)$$

(using the binomial expansion)

$$= \left(\frac{n_1}{n_2}+\frac{e_1}{n_2}\right)\left(1-\frac{e_2}{n_2}\right)$$

$$= \frac{n_1}{n_2}+\frac{e_1}{n_2}-\frac{e_1e_2}{(n_2)^2}-\frac{e_2n_1}{(n_2)^2}.$$

As with the corresponding work in multiplication, we can ignore the term in e_1e_2 and calculate the relative error:

$$\simeq \left| \frac{e_1}{n_2} - \frac{e_2 n_1}{(n_2)^2} \right| \bigg/ \left| \frac{n_1}{n_2} \right|$$

$$= \left| \frac{e_1}{n_1} - \frac{e_2}{n_2} \right|$$

$$\leqslant \left| \frac{e_1}{n_1} \right| + \left| \frac{e_2}{n_2} \right|.$$

The result is therefore the same as that for multiplication, i.e. the relative error is less than the sum of the relative errors of the original approximations. Here again, a purely arithmetic demonstration will be of the most value.

example 7 Divide 3·5 by 2·7 (two sig. fig.).
The 'worst cases' are when the errors in the numerator and denominator are of opposite signs. Thus the answer can lie between:

$$\frac{3\cdot45}{2\cdot75} \quad \text{and} \quad \frac{3\cdot55}{2\cdot65}.$$

By desk machine, rounding each division to five sig. fig., we get:

$$\frac{3\cdot45}{2\cdot75} = 1\cdot2545$$

$$\frac{3\cdot5}{2\cdot7} = 1\cdot2963$$

$$\frac{3\cdot55}{2\cdot65} = 1\cdot3396.$$

Thus the maximum error is 0·043 (two sig. fig.) and the best answer is 1·3 to two significant figures.

The maximum relative errors in the numbers 2·7 and 3·5 are, as in example 6, 0·019 and 0·014 respectively. The maximum relative error in the quotient is given by:

$$\left| \frac{+0\cdot043}{1\cdot2963} \right| \simeq 0\cdot033,$$

showing that the relative error property is satisfied.

We may conclude that serious errors always occur when nearly equal numbers are subtracted on a machine of limited capacity, but in other operations the worst possible effect is a loss in the reliability of the least significant figure. However, if a series of arithmetic operations are performed on the same data, then the errors in each of the basic operations will tend to accumulate, and answers in such cases should be viewed with caution.

4.8 error accumulation in lengthy computations

The following examples show how programming techniques can avoid errors accumulating during a series of arithmetic operations.

example 8 (Pythagoras' theorem) We require to find the third side of a right-angled triangle given the hypotenuse and one other side. If the sides of the triangle are p, q and r, then we require to compute r from the formula

$$r = \sqrt{(p^2 - q^2)}.$$

Consider the problem of computing $p^2 - q^2$ when $p = 3 \cdot 2$ and $q = 2 \cdot 8$ on a machine which rounds each intermediate answer to two decimal digits. If we use the flow chart in fig. 10, the computation proceeds as follows:

$A \leftarrow 3 \cdot 2 \times 3 \cdot 2 = 10$ (two sig. fig.)
$B \leftarrow 2 \cdot 8 \times 2 \cdot 8 = 7 \cdot 8$ (two sig. fig.)
$C \leftarrow 10 - 7 \cdot 8 = 2 \cdot 2$ (assuming that accuracy is not lost during the lining-up process).

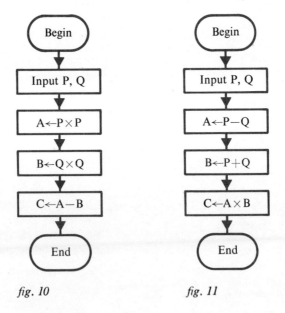

fig. 10   *fig. 11*

If, however, fig. 11 is used, we get:

$A \leftarrow 3 \cdot 2 - 2 \cdot 8 = 0 \cdot 4$
$B \leftarrow 3 \cdot 2 + 2 \cdot 8 = 6 \cdot 0$
$C \leftarrow 0 \cdot 4 \times 6 \cdot 0 = 2 \cdot 4$.

Working exactly, the value of C is $10 \cdot 24 - 7 \cdot 84 = 2 \cdot 40$ showing that the first method gives a percentage relative error of 10 per cent whereas the second is accurate in both significant figures.

example 9 (The quadratic equation) If a formula method is used to solve the quadratic equation:

$$x^2 - 24x + 1 = 0,$$

we have to compute:

$$x = 12 \pm \sqrt{143}.$$

If the square root, 11·96, is found to four sig. fig., the values of x are found to be:

$$12 + 11 \cdot 96 = 23 \cdot 96$$
$$\text{and} \quad 12 - 11 \cdot 96 = 0 \cdot 04.$$

These answers are of very different relative accuracy, having four and one significant figures respectively. The error in the smaller root may be reduced by using the fact that the product of the roots is 1, and so may be calculated from the reciprocal 1/23·96 giving 0·04174, which is correct in all four figures. This method of 'error control' gives a dramatic increase in the relative accuracy of the roots.

4.9 conclusion

The earlier examples have shown the effect of working with the maximum error at each stage, and in practice, some of these errors will tend to cancel each other out. It is essential, however, that pupils are made aware of such errors, so that they treat results from a computer with caution, and do not develop the blind faith that 'the computer is always right'. A computational device can only work to a fixed degree of accuracy, and to a method which is defined by the programmer. If this method is poor, then the programmer, not the computer, must be blamed for the resulting inaccuracies.

5 generation of sequences

5.1 introduction

In this chapter we shall be considering mainly recurrence relations and sequences, but at the same time taking the chance to digress and follow up some interesting properties.

We begin with a problem which it is hoped will not seem too contrived to merit serious attention. The harder related problem leads to a flow chart which demonstrates well the power of a computer in finding a solution by trial and error. These problems take us on to recurrence relations and the sequences defined by them. Among the examples considered in detail are the Fibonacci sequence and Pascal's Triangle. Prime numbers lead to many sequences and it is hoped that here, as elsewhere, the teacher will find the germ of other ideas. This is followed by a discussion of the definition of a sequence and its limit. The derivative in calculus is based on the all-important idea of a limit and arises naturally from this chapter's basic practical work.

5.2 introductory problems

problem A boy has a wealthy uncle, who opens a special bank account for him by putting in £0·10. He says to the boy, 'You may take money out of the bank but you must not pay money in. At the end of each month for the period of one year, I will double the amount you have in the bank at that stage.' If the boy were to decide not to touch the money at all, how much would the uncle have to pay in at the end of each month? The uncle knows his nephew well, however, and reckons that the more money the boy has in the bank, the more he will spend. He has therefore based his calculations on his nephew's spending one-quarter of his bank balance during each month. What happens if the boy spends one-half of his bank balance each month? Also what happens if the uncle's calculations are correct?

solution

(1) Assuming the boy spends nothing at all, then at the end of the first month the amount becomes £0·20. After the second month the amount is £0·40, after three months it is £0·80, and so on. The amount in the bank at any stage during the year is essentially represented by the program instruction $X \leftarrow 2X$. This gives rise to the following straightforward flow chart to calculate the bank balance at the end of any month (see fig. 1).

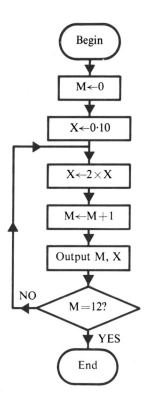

M = the number of the month

X = the total amount in £s
in the bank after M months

fig. 1

If the boy were to take nothing out of the bank, the bank balance at the end of the year is the total amount the uncle has to pay out altogether (a rather large amount!).

(2) In the case where the boy spends half of his monthly balance, it is not difficult to see that his uncle has to pay in only £0·05 each month.

(3) Now we consider the case where the boy regularly spends one-quarter of his monthly balance. He starts the first month with £0·10, spends £0·02$\frac{1}{2}$ and ends the month with £0·07$\frac{1}{2}$ which his uncle doubles to make £0·15. Suppose, at a later stage, the boy has £x at the start of a month. He spends £$\frac{1}{4}x$ and ends the month with £$\frac{3}{4}x$ in the bank; his uncle doubles this to make £$\frac{3}{2}x$. Thus an amount £x at the beginning of a month becomes £$\frac{3}{2}x$ at the beginning of the next month or, as this will appear in our flow chart 'X←1·5X'. The flow chart continues along lines similar to fig. 1.

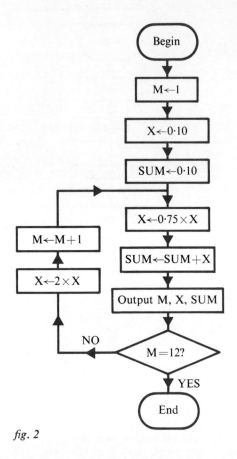

fig. 2

Now we see how much it has cost the uncle in this case and write a flow chart (fig. 2) to show the month M, the money X paid in at the end of that month, and the running total of money so far paid in which we call SUM.

It is a valuable exercise for the pupil to consider what location X contains at each stage of the flow chart.

It is interesting to consider what difference it makes if the boy rashly spends £0·05 in the first month and then, realising his error, spends one-quarter of his balance during the remaining months.

problem (more advanced) Suppose, instead, the uncle had said to the boy, 'I am putting £0·10 in a special account for you. At the end of each month I will double the amount remaining in the bank until the end of the twelfth month when whatever remains in the account becomes mine again. You are to choose a certain fixed fraction and spend this fraction of your bank balance each month.' What fraction should the boy choose in order to make the most of his uncle's offer?

solution Let the fixed fraction be k. Clearly, if $k=0$ the money stays untouched in the bank until it is reclaimed by the uncle and the boy gets nothing.
If $k=1$ the boy gets £0·10 in the first month and nothing else after that.
If $k=\frac{1}{2}$ he gets £0·05 each month, making only £0·60 in all.
The boy quickly realises that any value of k between $\frac{1}{2}$ and 1 gives him less than £0·60 in all, but cannot see which is the best value of k between 0 and $\frac{1}{2}$ to take.
A friendly sixth former tries to solve the problem by using calculus but finds it is too difficult. A friend who is a skilled programmer suggests the flow chart of fig. 3 to put on a computer.

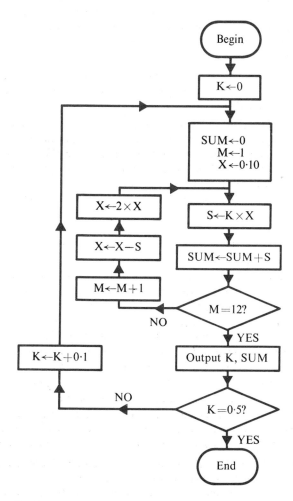

fig. 3

This flow chart tests values of k from 0 to 0·5 in steps of 0·1, giving the corresponding total withdrawn. From these results a smaller range of values of k can be chosen for further investigation in a similar flow chart changing k in steps of 0·01. Alternatively the instruction 'K←K+0·01' could have been inserted instead of 'K←K+0·1'. Depending on the computer facilities available this may well be the better method.

5.3 recurrence relations

In the flow charts in figs. 1, 2 and 3 we have inserted an instruction of the form X←2×X, SUM←SUM+S, M←M+1. We are using an existing value of the variable to calculate a new value and this process is repeated as many times as we require. To avoid using too much storage space in a computer, it is a necessary technique to use the same address for consecutive values of the variable.

It is sometimes useful to give each value of a variable a separate label. This is conveniently done by the use of suffixes. For example, successive values of a variable x can be called $x_1, x_2, \ldots x_{20}, \ldots$, etc.

The relations between these terms in the case of X←2X are now $x_2 = 2x_1$, $x_3 = 2x_2, \ldots x_{20} = 2x_{19}$, and so on. These results can be summarised by $x_{n+1} = 2x_n$ where n can take any positive integral value. Such an equation is known as a *recurrence relation*. Here we need to know only the value of x_1 in order to find as many of the x_n as we like, e.g. if $x_1 = 3$, then $x_2 = 2 \times 3 = 6$, $x_3 = 2 \times 6 = 12$, etc. Thus we have built up a sequence of xs, namely 3, 6, 12, 24 . . . .

5.4 Fibonacci sequence

A recurrence relation need not connect only two consecutive terms – many important ones connect three or more terms. There is a well-known sequence of numbers which starts 1, 1, 2, 3, 5, 8, 13 . . . . Its recurrence relation is, of course, $x_n = x_{n-1} + x_{n-2}$ (or some equivalent form such as $x_{n+2} = x_{n+1} + x_n$). This is the Fibonacci sequence. Note that the recurrence relation by itself does not tell us what the sequence is. We need to know in addition the first two terms x_1 and x_2. Alternative values of x_1 and x_2 give other sequences. For the Fibonacci sequence we want $x_1 = x_2 = 1$.

This sequence occurs in many situations in nature, including the growth pattern of a tree, rabbit populations and genetic theory, where it is interesting to note that, as Mendel discovered, the hereditary make-up of a generation is dependent not only upon the parents but also upon the grandparents.

The accompanying flow chart (fig. 4) will output Fibonacci numbers indefinitely. Adapt it so that it will calculate: the first thirty Fibonacci numbers; Fibonacci numbers less than 10 000. For further properties of Fibonacci numbers see the problems at the end of this chapter.

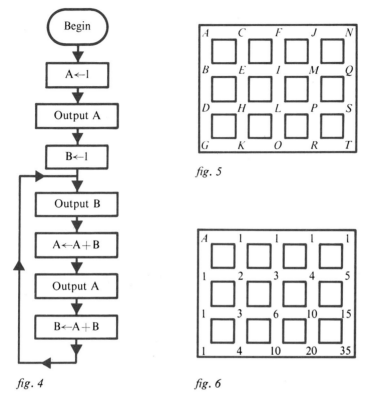

fig. 4

fig. 5

fig. 6

5.5 Pascal's Triangle

There are many ways of introducing the array of numbers, which occurs frequently in mathematics, known as Pascal's Triangle. We give here one of the more unusual approaches which makes good use of a recurrence relation similar to the one used in generating the Fibonacci sequence. In fact, we shall see that there is a connection between the two sets of numbers.

Fig. 5 represents twelve blocks of flats forming a regular pattern, and the paths between them. A man leaves A to meet a friend at T. He takes one of the shortest routes. How many such routes are there?

The problem is best approached by counting the number of shortest routes to each of the junctions $B, C, D, \ldots T$ in turn and inserting this number at the appropriate junction. Obviously there is only one way to get to B and to C. So we put a 1 at each of B and C. To get to E the man can go via C or via B: thus there are two ways, and we put a 2 at E. There is only one way to D and F and, for that matter, to G, J and N. To get to H he must go via D or E. Having arrived at D or E there is only one way to get to H. Therefore the number of ways of getting to H is the sum of the number of ways of getting to D and the number of ways of getting to E, i.e. $1+2=3$ ways. Hence we can put a 3 at *H* and similarly a 3 at *I*. We continue in this way to obtain the numbers in fig. 6 and the answer to our problem is 35. We have been using a recurrence relation, e.g. referring back to fig. 5

the number at $L+$ the number at $M=$ the number at P, etc.

The connection between this problem and the well-known Pascal's Triangle is easily seen in fig. 7.

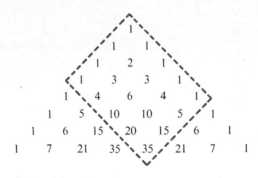

fig. 7

Thus the problem of finding the number of shortest paths for a different rectangular (or square) pattern of such blocks will involve finding the appropriate number in a row of Pascal's Triangle.

To assist in writing a flow chart for this we shall arrange the triangle as shown in fig. 8.

```
1
1   1
1   2   1
1   3   3   1
1   4   6   4   1
1   5   10  10  5   1
------------------------
```

fig. 8

It can be seen that any number (apart from the 1 at the top) is the sum of two numbers in the row above, viz. the number immediately above it and the number diagonally to the left. Where there is no such number, treat it as a zero. We now consider a flow chart to generate a particular row of the Pascal Triangle and take the sixth row as an example to give the general idea. First we observe that this row contains six numbers (elements). We start from the 1 of the first row and extend the first row by introducing five zeros so that we get:

     1 0 0 0 0 0.

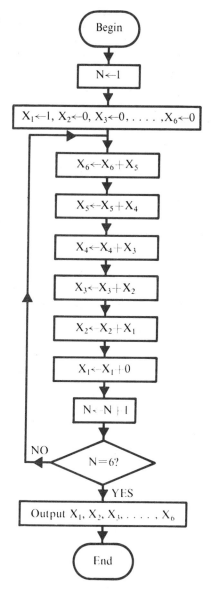

fig. 9

In our flow chart (fig. 9) we shall overwrite this row with successive rows of Pascal's Triangle until we obtain row 6.

If x_1, x_2, x_3, ... and y_1, y_2, y_3 ... are the elements of successive rows of the triangle, we have $y_3 = x_3 + x_2$ and, in general, $y_n = x_n + x_{n-1}$. Since we are overwriting, this will appear as the instruction '$X_N \leftarrow X_N + X_{N-1}$' and our initial values of the xs are $x_1 = 1$, $x_2 = x_3 = x_4 = x_5 = x_6 = 0$.

The teacher should emphasise that the first calculation instruction is $X_6 \leftarrow X_6 + X_5$, i.e. we are calculating from the right-hand end of each row. Ask why it is disastrous to start at the left-hand end with $X_1 \leftarrow X_1 + 0$, $X_2 \leftarrow X_2 + X_1$, $X_3 \leftarrow X_3 + X_2$, etc.

Clearly each row could have been output as it was calculated, if this had been required, simply by including the output statement in the loop. To generate rows beyond the sixth we should need more xs at the beginning with $x_1 = 1$ and all the other xs equal to zero.

If we require, say, the twentieth row, it would be cumbersome to have twenty recurrence relations in our flow diagram. There is a more sophisticated device which is an extension of that used in one of the sorting programs in chapter 3 and which appreciably shortens the flow chart.

The flow chart which follows (fig. 11) calculates the nth row of the Pascal Triangle. The value of n must be assigned at the beginning and, as before, the initial values of the xs are $x_1 = 1$ and the rest are zero.

To avoid difficulty with our instruction $X_I \leftarrow X_I + X_{I-1}$ we must not allow I to take the value 1 (otherwise we shall be referring to X_0 which is undefined). It would thus appear that x_1 has not been calculated. We have used the fact that x_1 is always 1.

An interesting property of the Pascal Triangle arranged as in fig. 10 is that if we sum the terms diagonally as shown we obtain the Fibonacci sequence. A program to generate the Fibonacci numbers by using this property involves a subtle use of subscripted variables but should not be beyond the powers of a good fifth- or sixth-form pupil.

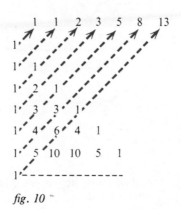

fig. 10

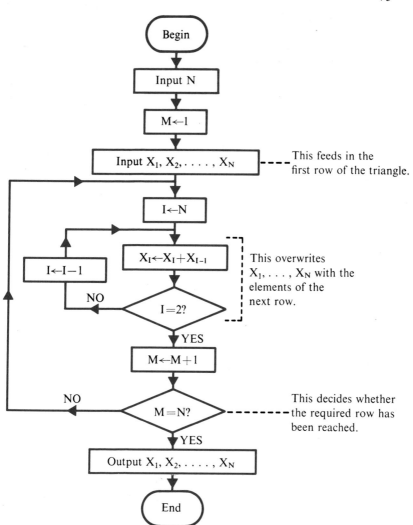

fig. 11

74

5.6 factorials and combinations

At this point it is necessary to introduce a symbol to denote such calculations as $4 \times 3 \times 2 \times 1$ and $5 \times 4 \times 3 \times 2 \times 1$. This symbol is $n!$ (read as n factorial) and defined as $n \times (n-1) \times (n-2) \times \ldots \times 3 \times 2 \times 1$.

Fig. 12 is a flow chart showing the process by which a computer could calculate $n!$

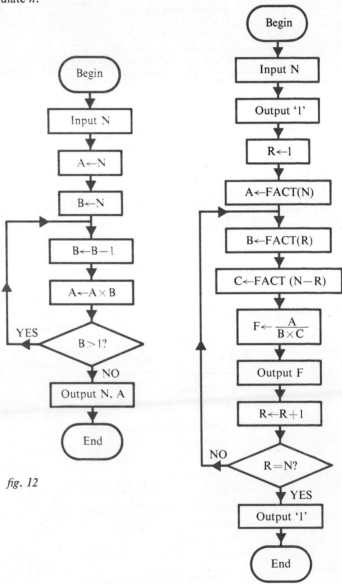

fig. 12

fig. 13

Using the factorial notation combinations are defined by:

$$^nC_r \quad \text{or} \quad \binom{n}{r} = \frac{n!}{(n-r)!r!}.$$

Space does not permit us to develop this topic further but having dealt with combinations (and permutations) in the usual way and linked them to a study of probability the teacher should not miss the opportunity to link up the $(n+1)$th row of Pascal's Triangle with the binomial expansion of $(a+b)^n$ and also to show that these coefficients are also the ^nC_r where r takes values from 0 to n (0! being defined as 1).

Fig. 13 is a flow chart to print out the $(n+1)$th row of Pascal's Triangle, using combinations and calls upon fig. 12 as a subroutine which it calls FACT.

5.7 another example of a recurrence relation

Triangular numbers, t_n, are defined as the number of dots needed to make up each triangle of the sequence of equilateral triangles in fig. 14. Clearly $t_2=t_1+2$ since we get from t_1 to t_2 by adding 2 dots. Then $t_3=t_2+3$ since we get from t_2 to t_3 by adding 3 dots. Hence $t_{n+1}=t_n+(n+1)$ and this result together with $t_1=1$ will generate all the triangular numbers as far as the nth as shown in fig. 15.

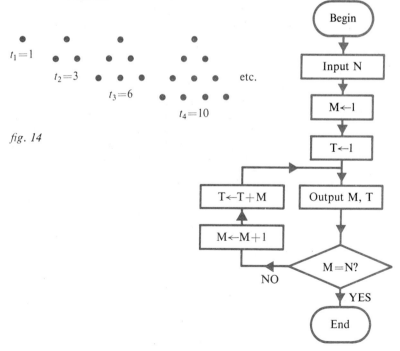

fig. 14

fig. 15

5.8 prime numbers

If we truncate 12·34 by removing the decimal part to obtain 12, then 12 is called the integer part of 12·34. Similarly, the integer part of 239·7621 is 239. This we shall write as INT(239·7621)=239. For what type of number x does INT$(x)=x$? Obviously x has to be an integer.

Some computers are equipped with a function INT which is invaluable when, in a program, we want to test if a number p is exactly divisible by q. We calculate $x=p\div q$ and then ask if $x=$INT(x); only if $x=$INT(x) is p divisible by q.

example

a Is 102 divisible by 13?   **b** Is 91 divisible by 7?

In **a** the computer is asked to work out $102\div 13$ which it will store in X as 7·846153 ... depending on the capacity of the store. INT$(x)=7$. Thus INT$(x)\neq x$ and so 102 is not divisible by 13.

In **b** $91\div 7$ is stored in X as 13 and also INT$(x)=13$. Thus, as INT$(x)=x$, we have found that 7 is a factor of 91.

We shall make use of these ideas in a flow chart to test whether or not an integer x is prime, making use of the fact that if x can be factorised, it must have at least one factor (other than 1) less than or equal to $\sqrt{x}$ (see fig. 16).

Since it is obvious that an even number greater than 2 is not prime we need test only odd numbers in our flow chart. The process can thus be speeded up by replacing the instruction K←K+1 by K←K+2 and changing the initial k to 3.

but – we have a difficulty!

Suppose that the computer were to test the largest known prime, i.e. $2^{11213}-1$ by this method, leaving aside the storage problems of such large numbers. It is interesting to see how long it would take. Let us assume that the time taken for one loop is 1/1 000 000 sec. We would require $2^{11213/2}$ loops, i.e. approximately 2^{5600}. The time taken is then $2^{5600}/(10^6\times 3600\times 24\times 365)$ years which is of the order of 10^{1670} years. Some other method would therefore be essential!

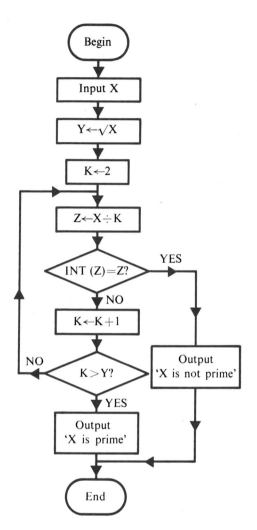

fig. 16

We end this section with a flow chart (fig. 17) which will output all the factors of an integer x including itself and 1. This will be useful in answering the question on perfect numbers at the end of this chapter.

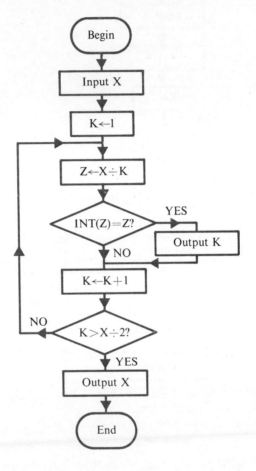

fig. 17

5.9 sequences and limits

We define a *sequence* as an unending set of terms listed in a definite order, i.e. as a mapping of the domain of natural numbers 1, 2, 3, ... where the image of the number n is the nth term of the sequence.

If you were asked to calculate 2^{12} it is likely that you would go through the terms of the following sequence in your mind: 2, 4, 8, 16, 32, 64, 128, 256, 512, 1024, 2048, 4096, ... keeping count of the power as you go. For 2^{12} you would stop at 4096. If we go on further the numbers get bigger and bigger, eventually exceeding any number that we care to mention.

Another simple sequence is $\dfrac{1}{2}, \dfrac{3}{4}, \dfrac{7}{8}, \dfrac{15}{16}, \dfrac{31}{32}$, ... (where the pattern suggested by the first five terms is continued). The terms of this sequence also increase in size but this time we can choose a number greater than any term which can arise in the sequence, for instance 10, or 2, or 1. It would seem (and it can be proved) that we cannot afford to go lower than 1. We say that the *limit* of this sequence is 1, because as we progress along the sequence, its terms get closer to 1 than they do to any other number. When a sequence has a limit (necessarily finite) we say that it is a *convergent* sequence or that the sequence converges.

More rigorously, if I say that a sequence $s_1, s_2, s_3,$ ... converges to a limit s (written $s_n \to s$ as $n \to \infty$) then, however small a positive number you choose, I must be able to state the term in the sequence after which the numerical difference between every succeeding term and the limit s is smaller than the number you chose. It is very important that you choose first as my choice of term is based upon your choice.

Other examples of convergent sequences are $2\frac{1}{2}, 1\frac{3}{4}, 2\frac{1}{8}, 1\frac{5}{16}, 2\frac{1}{32}, 1\frac{63}{64},$ ... and $2\frac{1}{4}, 2\frac{1}{5}, 2\frac{1}{6}, 2\frac{1}{7},$ ... which both converge to the limit 2.

Our first example, where $s_n = 2^n$, is a divergent sequence. Other examples of sequences which do not converge are:

1, 2, 3, 1, 2, 3, 1, 2, 3, ... and
1, −2, 3, −4, 5, ...

In the examples on limits which follow at the end of this chapter, by the nature of a computer, we are working to a restricted number of decimal places. If, therefore, a sequence has a limit we shall expect all the terms to be 'equal' after a certain stage. The converse, unfortunately, cannot always be relied upon, but we can take this 'equality' of terms as a fairly reliable indication that there is a limit which has thus been found to within the permitted accuracy.

example Discover the rule for generating terms of the sequence

$$\frac{1}{1}, \frac{3}{2}, \frac{7}{5}, \frac{17}{12}, \frac{41}{29}, \frac{99}{70}, \dots$$

and find the limit of this sequence correct to four decimal places.

solution The solution of this problem is given in fig. 18.
Only the first four decimal places of the output S_i should be accepted. It may be proved that the sequence converges to $\sqrt{2}$ and so here we should obtain 1·4142 as our solution.

5.10 gradient of tangent to a curve as the limit of a sequence

The concept of a sequence and a limit is a very important and far-reaching one in mathematics. The computer may be used well to demonstrate how the limit of a sequence of gradients of chords on a curve may be seen to give the gradient of a tangent. A general proof would then be more convincing to the pupil who would otherwise be worried by the apparent $0 \div 0$ which somehow gives the gradient of a tangent.

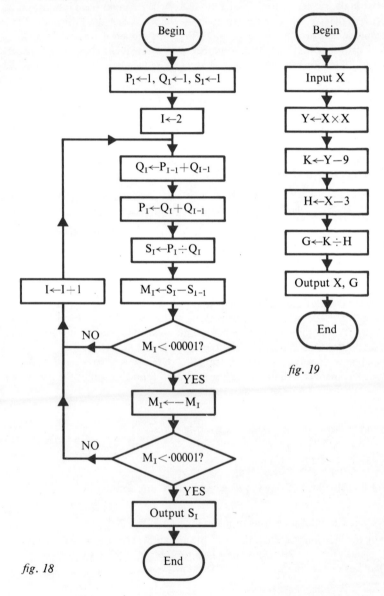

fig. 18

fig. 19

The general idea may be grasped by considering the curve $y=x^2$. Our aim is to find the gradient of the tangent to this curve at the point (3, 9) by finding the common limit of the sequence of gradients of the chords PQ_1, PQ_2, PQ_3, PQ_4, ... and of the chords PR_1, PR_2, PR_3, PR_4, ...

By using the flow chart of fig. 19 the two tables fig. 21 and fig. 22 may be completed and the limit of the sequence of gradients of PQ_n and of PR_n may be observed as 6 in both cases.

N.B. In fig. 19 do not try to feed in the value $x=3$. Why?

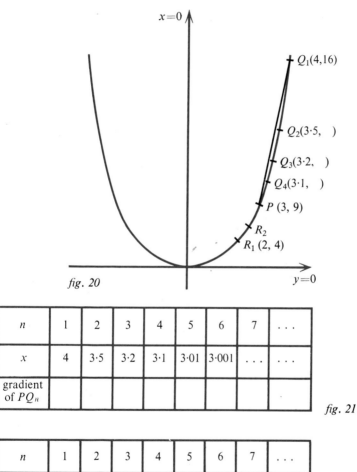

fig. 20

n	1	2	3	4	5	6	7	...	
x	4	3·5	3·2	3·1	3·01	3·001	...	...	
gradient of PQ_n									

fig. 21

n	1	2	3	4	5	6	7	...	
x	2	2·5	2·8	2·9	2·99	...	...	...	
gradient of PR_n									

fig. 22

After the above discussion the pupil should be more ready for a calculus proof on the following lines:

Since $Q(h, k)$ lies on the curve $y = x^2$

then $9 + k = (3 + h)^2$

$9 + k = 9 + 6h + h^2$

$k = 6h + h^2$

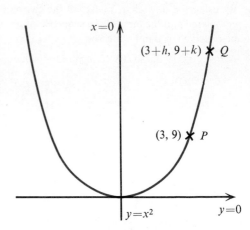

fig. 23

Now the gradient of the chord PQ (whether Q is above P or below it)

$$= k \div h$$
$$= \frac{6h + h^2}{h}$$
$$= 6 + h.$$

As Q moves along the curve towards P, h gets smaller and tends to zero. In the limit, the gradient of the chord $PQ \to 6$. Hence the gradient of the tangent at $P = 6$.

The next stage now might be to take P as the general point (x, y) on the curve $y = x^2$ with Q as $(x + \delta x, y + \delta y)$, or its equivalent, and finally on to gradients at any point on a wide variety of curves.

examples

1   Write a flow chart to output the value of 2^n.

2   **a** Write a flow chart to evaluate $1 + 1/n$ for values of n from 1 to 20.
   b Write a flow chart to evaluate $(1 + 1/n)^n$ for values of n from 1 to 20.

The sequence of values of $(1 + 1/n)^n$ converges very slowly to the value which is called e in higher mathematics, $e = 2 \cdot 71828 \ldots$.

3   There is a very interesting connection between the Fibonacci numbers and the 'golden mean', i.e. $\frac{1}{2}(1 + \sqrt{5})$. It is that the sequence $\dfrac{1}{1}, \dfrac{2}{1}, \dfrac{3}{2}, \dfrac{5}{3}, \dfrac{8}{5}, \cdots$

(notice the Fibonacci numbers) has as its limit the golden mean. Write a flow chart to evaluate the first twenty ratios and to evaluate also $\frac{1}{2}(1 + \sqrt{5})$.

4   In fact, the ratios of consecutive terms of any sequence which obeys $x_n = x_{n-1} + x_{n-2}$ will tend to the golden mean. Try this out for the sequence 5, 2, 7, 9, ... by evaluating the first twenty of the sequence $\frac{2}{5}, \frac{7}{2}, \frac{9}{7}, \ldots$ It does not matter if a finite number of mistakes is made in calculating these ratios!

5   Write a flow chart to evaluate the first four Fermat numbers of the sequence given by $2^{2^n} + 1$ given by $n = 0, 1, 2, 3$. These are prime numbers. The value $n = 4$ gives a composite number and it is likely (but has never been proved) that there are no further Fermat primes. The Fermat primes have applications to perfect numbers and to the ruler and compass constructions of regular polygons.

6   Perfect numbers are positive integers whose factors, including 1 but not the number itself, add up to the number. The first perfect number is 6 since $3 + 2 + 1 = 6$. The second is 28 since $1 + 2 + 4 + 7 + 14 = 28$. These numbers were originally thought to have a mystic significance. Write a flow chart which will test integers up to n to see if they are perfect numbers. (Fig. 17 should be adapted and extended.)

7   If one term of a sequence of positive terms is $\frac{m}{n}$ and the next is $\frac{m+2n}{m+n}$ i.e. $\frac{m}{n} \to \frac{m+2n}{m+n}$, prove mathematically that the limit of such a sequence is $\sqrt{2}$.

Write a flow chart to output the first n terms of the sequence $\frac{1}{1}, \frac{3}{2}, \frac{7}{5}, \frac{17}{12}, \ldots$

8   Cannon balls are piled up so as to form a triangular pyramid. The number in the nth layer from the top is of course, t_n, the nth triangular number. If s_n represents the total number of cannon balls from the top down to and including the nth layer, find a connection between s_n, s_{n-1} and t_n. Use this connection to write a flow chart which will calculate s_n for any given n.

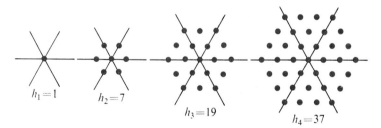

9   The above diagram shows how we may generate numbers called hexagonal numbers. Depicted are the first four numbers of the sequence h_n. Write a flow chart to display the first n of these hexagonal numbers.

10   Repeat the above question for the first n pentagonal numbers $p_n = 1$, 6, 16, ... defined in a similar way.

11   Devise a flow chart on the lines of the discussion in section 5.10 to find the gradient of the tangent at: **a** the point (2, 10) on the curve $y = 3x^2 - 2x + 2$; **b** the point (3, 27) on the curve $y = x^3$.

6 series

6.1 introduction

The study of series, both finite and infinite, has long been regarded as a sixth-form topic. We hope to show here that the much less abstract approach afforded by the computer enables us usefully to introduce this work at an earlier stage. The emphasis here is on experiment and inductive reasoning.

We begin the chapter with a piece of work readily accepted by eleven-year-olds.

$$1 = 1 = 1^2$$
$$1+3 = 4 = 2^2$$
$$1+3+5 = 9 = 3^2$$
$$1+3+5+7 = 16 = 4^2$$

There seems to be some evidence that if we take the first six odd numbers, their sum will be 36 and this may be easily verified. Is this always true? i.e. is the sum of the first n odd numbers $= n^2$?

We have tested this for small values of n. The flow chart in fig. 1 shows how larger values of n may be tried. The flow chart is devised to give the output n, the value of n^2 and the sum of the first n odd numbers.

The results of our flow chart indicate that our suspicions are confirmed. To a mathematician this would not constitute a proof, but an important step towards a proof by mathematical induction.

The flow chart can very easily be adapted to answer such questions as 'What is the sum if the last term is 31?'

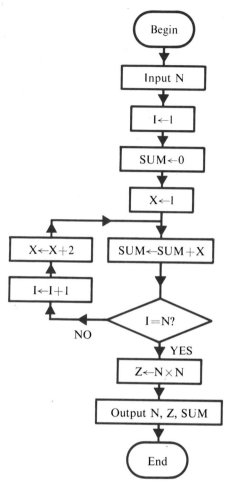

fig 1.

86

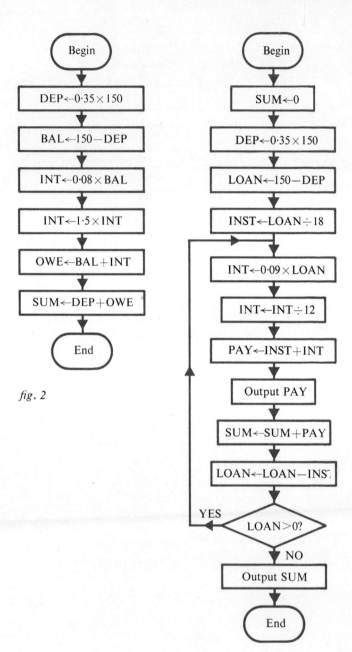

Begin

DEP←0·35×150

BAL←150−DEP

INT←0·08×BAL

INT←1·5×INT

OWE←BAL+INT

SUM←DEP+OWE

End

fig. 2

Begin

SUM←0

DEP←0·35×150

LOAN←150−DEP

INST←LOAN÷18

INT←0·09×LOAN

INT←INT÷12

PAY←INST+INT

Output PAY

SUM←SUM+PAY

LOAN←LOAN−INST

LOAN>0?

YES

NO

Output SUM

End

fig. 3

6.2 hire purchase

A boy wishes to buy a motor scooter which is on sale at a nearby shop for £150. The shop is asking hire purchase terms of a 35 per cent deposit with the balance to be paid in eighteen equal monthly instalments. The interest is the same each month and is charged at the rate of 8 per cent per year of the original 65 per cent debt. Calculate how much the scooter costs if bought in this way (see fig. 2).

A garage offers the same model for the same cost, again asking for a 35 per cent deposit with the balance to be paid in eighteen monthly instalments. The interest this time is charged at 9 per cent per year based on the loan outstanding after each month. Which offer is the better? (See fig. 3.)

The two offers may now be compared and it is easy to see which the boy should accept.

As an exercise the pupil could be asked to put a counter into fig. 3 so that the output called PAY in the loop could be coupled with the number of the month.

The pupils might then go on to consider other similar examples such as building-society loans, bank loans, taxation, stocks and shares.

6.3 sequences and series

In everyday life the words sequence and series are used interchangeably. In mathematics each has a precise and distinct meaning. In the last chapter we defined a sequence as an unending set of terms in a definite order such that each term can be calculated from either a knowledge of its position or a knowledge of the preceding terms. A sequence is an ordered mapping of the natural numbers.

In the example in section 6.1 we considered the sequence 1, 3, 5, 7, 9, ... and formed the sums of different numbers of terms, 1, $1+3$, $1+3+5$, $1+3+5+7$, etc. When we add terms of a sequence together in this fashion we form a series and our flow chart calculates the sum of various such series.

We saw that 1, $1+3$, $1+3+5$, $1+3+5+7$, ... were 1^2, 2^2, 3^2, 4^2, ... and these if carried on indefinitely form a sequence. So the study of the sum of a series comes down sometimes to the study of sequences, especially when the series is infinite.

6.4 Achilles and the tortoise

One of the first problems of this type was posed by Zeno. It concerns Achilles and the tortoise who were having a race. Achilles could run ten times as fast as the tortoise and so he gave the tortoise a 100 m start. Zeno argued that Achilles could never overtake the tortoise for, when he had run 100 m the tortoise had moved on 10 m, and when Achilles had covered this 10 m the tortoise was 1 m further on. At any time when Achilles reached a point where the tortoise had been, the tortoise had moved on further. Hence Achilles could never overtake the tortoise!

The flow chart in fig. 4 shows how far Achilles had moved at each stage of the argument. We know that when Achilles had run 120 m for example, the tortoise had covered only 12 m and therefore the tortoise had already been overtaken.

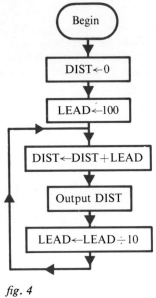

fig. 4

When Achilles had run s m the tortoise had run $s/10$ m and thus they were level when:

$s=100+s/10$

i.e. $s=111\frac{1}{9}$

Hence the infinite series:

$100+10+1+\cdot1+\cdot01+\cdot001+ \dots$

of the flow chart converges to the limit $111\frac{1}{9}$. The successive outputs would be the sequence 100, 110, 111, 111·1, 111·11, ...

More generally, if $u_1, u_2, u_3, u_4, \dots$ form a sequence, then $u_1+u_2+u_3+ \dots +u_n$ is a series and if we put $s_1=u_1$; $s_2=u_1+u_2$; $s_3=u_1+u_2+u_3, \dots$; $s_n=u_1+u_2+u_3+ \dots +u_n$ then $s_1, s_2, s_3, \dots , s_n \dots$ form a new sequence. If the sequence $s_1, s_2, s_3, \dots , s_n$, has a limit s then we say that the infinite series $u_1+u_2+ \dots +u_n+ \dots$ has a sum to infinity s, or that the series is convergent with s as the sum to infinity. Note that a sequence must be unending, but we shall be investigating both finite and infinite series. The terms of the sequence $1^2, 2^2 3^2, \dots$ increase without limit and we say that the corresponding infinite series $1+3+5+7+ \dots$ is divergent (rather than say the sum to infinity is infinite).

6.5 finite series

What have the following three series in common?

$$1+2+3+ 4+ \ldots +20$$
$$2+5+8+11+ \ldots +32$$
$$\tfrac{1}{2}+2+3\tfrac{1}{2}+5+ \ldots +15\tfrac{1}{2}$$

If each term of a series is obtained by adding a fixed amount to the previous term, then we call the series an arithmetic progression (AP).

Note that $7+5+3+1-1-3$ is also an AP. We are adding -2 each time.

Now consider the series:

$$1+2+4+8+16+ \ldots +256$$
$$2+6+18+54+ \quad \ldots +1458$$
$$81+27+9+ \qquad \ldots + \frac{1}{243}.$$

Here each term is obtained by multiplying the previous term by a fixed number. Such a series is called a geometric progression (GP). Note that $8-4+2-1+\tfrac{1}{2}-\tfrac{1}{4}$ is also a GP. We are multiplying by $-\tfrac{1}{2}$ this time. The theory of the AP and GP is treated in most standard works on algebra. The following approach, however, might be tried.

6.6 arithmetic progression

Write a flow chart to generate the first ten terms of the series $2+5+8+11+ \ldots$ As each term is found output the number of terms so far generated, the average of the first and last terms and the sum of all the terms so far found.

The pupil should be asked to tabulate his results and to try to find a connection between these three quantities. He should then try out the sum of, say, twenty-nine, thirty-five and fifty terms to see if his ideas are correct.

Clearly the flow chart in fig. 5 can be adapted to cope with all APs to any number of terms. The table of values of our flow chart here should be as in fig. 6.

It can be seen that $Sum = n \times Av$

i.e. $Sum = \dfrac{n(a+l)}{2}$,

where a and l are the first and last terms.

An alternative approach would be to calculate the average of the first and last terms, i.e. $(a+l)/2$ and the average term of the series i.e. $(Sum)/n$.

For an AP, of course, these are equal and therefore

$$\frac{a+l}{2} = \frac{Sum}{n}$$

i.e. $Sum = \dfrac{n(a+l)}{2}$

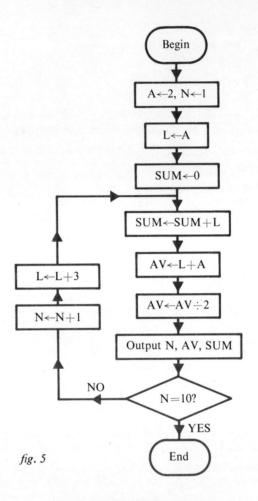

fig. 5

n	Av	Sum
1	2	2
2	$3\frac{1}{2}$	7
3	5	15
4	$6\frac{1}{2}$	26
5	8	40
6	$9\frac{1}{2}$	57
7	11	77
8	$12\frac{1}{2}$	100
9	14	126
10	$15\frac{1}{2}$	155

fig. 6

6.7 geometric progression

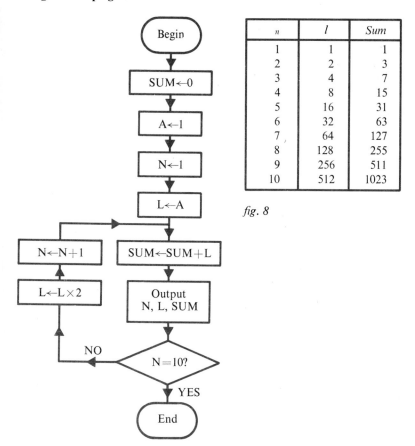

n	l	Sum
1	1	1
2	2	3
3	4	7
4	8	15
5	16	31
6	32	63
7	64	127
8	128	255
9	256	511
10	512	1023

fig. 8

fig. 7

Fig. 7 shows a flow chart to generate the first ten terms of the series $1+2+4+ \ldots +512$. As each term is found, output the number of terms so far, the last term and the sum of the terms so far found. These results should again be tabulated and conclusions drawn and tested by considering, say, twelve, twenty and twenty-six terms. The table of values of the flow chart should be as shown in fig. 8.

It should not escape notice that each value of *Sum* is one less than the following value for l (the last term) and the result $S_n = 2^n - 1$ should be obtained.

This suggests that for the series $1+3+9+27+ \ldots$ we should write a similar flow chart with the additional output of the value of $3^n - 1$. A table of values will show that $S_n = (3^n - 1)/2$ in this case.

Consideration of the series $1+4+16+64+$ ... will produce the result that $S_n=(4^n-1)/3$ and the general result $1+r+r^2+r^3+$ ... $+r^{n-1}=(r^n-1)/(r-1)$ may now be guessed at. Multiply this result throughout by a and we have the standard result for the sum of a GP:

i.e. $a+ar+ar^2+$ ... $+ar^{n-1}=a(r^n-1)/(r-1)$

which is sometimes more conveniently written $a(1-r^n)/(1-r)$.

6.8 infinite series

We turn our attention now to infinite series and to their convergence or otherwise. The GP is a good starting point.

For the series $1+2+2^2+2^3+2^4$ ... we have already seen that the sequence $s_1, s_2, s_3, s_4,$ ... where $s_1=1$, $s_2=1+2$, $s_3=1+2+2^2$, $s_4=1+2+2^2+2^3$, ... is 1, 3, 7, 15, 31, 63, 127, ... and that this is going to increase without limit, i.e. the sequence s_n has no limit, and the series $1+2+2^2+2^3$, ... therefore diverges. Now take the series $s_n=1+\frac{1}{2}+\frac{1}{4}+\frac{1}{8}+\frac{1}{16}+$ ... $+\frac{1}{2^{n-1}}$. A flow chart should be constructed by the pupil to calculate as many terms of the sequence $s_1, s_2, s_3, \ldots, s_{20},$ ... as is convenient. It will be seen that the sequence appears to have a limit of 2 or perhaps less, i.e. the series appears to converge.

We have a formula which gives the sum to n terms of any GP, i.e.

$s_n=a(r^n-1)/(r-1)$.

In our first example r was 2 and r^n therefore was 2^n which increases indefinitely as n increases. In our second example $r=\frac{1}{2}$ and $r^n=(\frac{1}{2})^n$ which gets nearer and nearer to zero as n increases so that in the limit where $n \to \infty$, $s_n \to 1(-1)/(\frac{1}{2}-1)=2$. Thus we have shown that $1+\frac{1}{2}+\frac{1}{4}+\frac{1}{8}+$ ... converges to the value 2.

In the case of the GP we are fortunate in having a simple expression for its sum from which it is easy to show whether or not the series converges. This is not usually the case for other types of infinite series.

Consider the infinite series:

$1+\frac{1}{2}+\frac{1}{3}+\frac{1}{4}$ ...

It is hard to believe that this series could ever exceed 100 but it does. Perhaps the most convincing 'proof' for the pupil is to program the sum to n terms and allow n to increase as far as possible. The sum increases extremely slowly but shows no sign of reaching a limit. The teacher should be warned however that in practice round-off errors soon have an appreciable effect on this demonstration. After such an exercise the pupil may more readily accept the standard proof of the divergence of this series.

This example will put the pupil on his guard against assuming that a series is convergent simply because its terms become progressively smaller and tend to zero.

If the series is $u_1+u_2+u_3+$ ... it cannot converge unless $u_n\to 0$ as $n\to\infty$; but the converse that if $u_n\to 0$ as $n\to\infty$ then the series converges is not necessarily true.

examples

1 Write a flow chart to add together the squares of the first n natural numbers. Design a loop to display the value of n, the value of the sum S_n where $S_n=1^2+2^2=3^2+$ ... $+n^2$ and the value of the expression

$$E_n=n(n+1)(2n+1)/6$$

letting n increase from 1 to 20. Compare S_n and E_n.

2 Repeat as in number 1 for:

	S_n	E_n
a	$1+2+3+$ ... $+n$	$\frac{1}{2}n(n+1)$
b	$1^3+2^3+3^3$ ... $+n^3$	$\frac{1}{4}n^2(n+1)^2$
c	$1+\frac{1}{2}+\frac{1}{4}+$ ... $+\dfrac{1}{2^n}$	$2-\dfrac{1}{2^{n-1}}$
d	$1.2+2.3+3.4+$ ... $+n(n+1)$	$\frac{1}{3}n(n+1)\,(n+2)$
e	$1.2.3+2.3.4+3.4.5+$ ... $+n(n+1)\,(n+2)$	$\frac{1}{4}n(n+1)\,(n+2)\,(n+3)$

3 Design a flow chart to sum the series:

$$1+\frac{1}{1!}+\frac{1}{2!}+\frac{1}{3!}+ \text{ ... } +\frac{1}{n!}$$

By considering the sum for increasing values of n look to see if this series has a limit. (This series converges to the number e which is approximately 2·71828.)

4 Series such as:

$$\frac{1}{1^2}+\frac{1}{2^2}+\frac{1}{3^2}+ \text{ ... } +\frac{1}{N^2}+ \text{ ... }$$

$$\frac{1}{1^3}+\frac{1}{2^3}+\frac{1}{3^3}+ \text{ ... } +\frac{1}{N^3}+ \text{ ... }$$

$$\frac{1}{1^4}+\frac{1}{2^4}+\frac{1}{3^4}+ \text{ ... } +\frac{1}{N^4}+ \text{ ... }$$

are all known to converge. In fact, it can be proved that

$$\frac{1}{1^p}+\frac{1}{2^p}+\frac{1}{3^p}+ \text{ ... } +\frac{1}{N^p}+ \text{ ... }$$

will converge provided $p>1$. (It will diverge if $p\leqslant 1$.)
Design flow charts to test for a limit to some of these series and see which values of p cause the series to converge quickly to its limit. When $p=2$ the limit is $\pi^2/6$.

5 The infinite series $1-\dfrac{1}{3}+\dfrac{1}{5}-\dfrac{1}{7}+\dfrac{1}{9}$ ... converges very slowly. The limit is $\frac{1}{4}\pi$. Design a flow chart to find the sum of as many terms as possible.

6   Another series which converges very slowly is $1-\frac{1}{2}+\frac{1}{3}-\frac{1}{4}+\frac{1}{5}-\frac{1}{6}$ ... The limit may be found as $\log_e 2$, i.e. approximately 0·69315.

7   When money is invested at compound interest, the interest at the end of the year, instead of being paid to the investor, is added to the amount invested and thus gains extra interest during the following year. Write a flow chart to output the amount an investor would have in the bank at the end of each year if he were to invest £250 at 3 per cent per year for ten years.

8   Write a flow chart to calculate for how many years you would have to invest £100 at $2\frac{1}{2}$ per cent per year compound interest if you wish at least to double your original investment. Adapt your flow chart to allow for different amounts of money, and for different percentage interest rates.

7 iteration

The development of the electronic computer has meant that numerical methods can play a greater part in the study of mathematics than was previously possible. The techniques themselves are not new, but the availability of high-speed computers has facilitated the understanding of such methods through practical experiment and demonstration. Pupils who have access to computers are inspired to invent their own techniques, and are able to embark on a programme of personal research into realistic problems without suffering from the deadening effect of a great burden of calculation.

This chapter is based on methods which were suggested and developed by a class of fifteen-year-old boys. All the examples are illustrations of solution by iteration, and sections 7.1 and 7.2 are a record of the work of two of these boys (P. Rank and N. Roberts, Cambridge Grammar School).

An iterative technique is one in which an estimate of the required solution is made, and this estimate is improved by trial until the required degree of accuracy is reached, each successive result being used in the next trial.

7.1 square roots

Suppose we wish to find the square root of 29. We know that 5^2 is 25, so we expect our square root to be more than 5. How much greater than 5? We might start by incrementing from 5 by intervals of 0·1, say, and squaring each time until our squared answer equals 29. If it exceeds 29 then we might revert to the previous value of the estimated square root and increment it only by 0·01. Manually this would be a slow process but on a computer it becomes quite rapid.

In the calculation of $\sqrt{29}$ which follows (fig. 1), an initial estimate of 5·1 is used and the incremental step is initially 0·1. Had an estimate of 6·0 been used (and found to be too large) it would be necessary to decrease our estimate by a suitable step. It would seem sensible, in this case, to go back to 5 and then to increment by 0·1.

A similar process could be used for the cube root or even the tenth root. The method is interesting. It was the way a boy tackled a problem without being told any more than 'Take the machine and find a square root without using the square root instruction.'

x	x^2	$x^2 > 29$?	Comment, if any
5·1	26·01	no	
5·2	27·04	no	
5·3	28·09	no	
5·4	29·16	yes	revert to 5·3 and increment by 0·01
5·31	28·1961	no	
5·32	28·3024	no	
5·33	28·4089	no	
5·34	28·5156	no	
5·35	28·6225	no	
5·36	28·7296	no	
5·37	28·8369	no	
5·38	28·9444	no	
5·39	29·0521	yes	revert to 5·38 and increment by 0·001
5·381	28·955161	no	
5·382	28·965924	no	
5·383	28·976689	no	
5·384	28·987456	no	
5·385	29·998225	no	
5·386	29·008996	yes	revert to 5·385 and increment by 0·0001

fig. 1

Another fascinating illustration of a simple iterative process displaying rapid convergence characteristics is that which uses the idea of the area of a square.

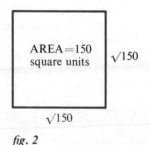

fig. 2

Suppose we wish to find $\sqrt{150}$, then if the area of a square were 150 square units, each side would represent $\sqrt{150}$ units exactly. If we had the good fortune to make a correct estimate for the square root of 150, then the result of dividing our guess into 150 should be equal to the estimate itself. If, however, the estimate were not correct, the quotient would differ. For example, a first estimate of 10 gives $150/10 = 15$.

Geometrically this represents a rectangle whose area is equal to the area of the desired square but whose sides are 10 and 15.

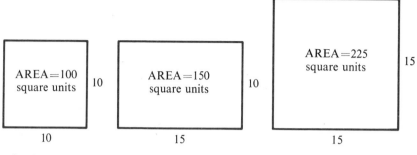

fig. 3

Fig. 3 shows us that $\sqrt{150}$ lies between 10 and 15 and we can therefore make another estimate somewhere between these two limits. An easy way of obtaining such an estimate is to use the mean of two numbers, in this case $\frac{1}{2}(10+15)$ $=12\cdot5$. Dividing 150 by this estimate gives $150/12\cdot5=12$. The rectangle of fig. 3 would now have sides 12, 12·5 (closer to a square) and as before we can obtain a new estimate of $x=\frac{1}{2}(12+12\cdot5)=12\cdot25$. On division, we find that $150/12\cdot25=12\cdot24$ (four sig. fig.) showing that $\sqrt{150}=12\cdot2$ correct to three significant figures (i.e. a value between 12·24 and 12·25).

The steps we have followed to obtain $x=\sqrt{n}$ are as follows:

(1) An initial approximation for x;
(2) A new estimate for x, using the previous estimate and obtained in the following way:

    a divide n by the estimate for x
    b calculate the average of the estimate and the result obtained in **a**
    c take this average to be the new estimate;

(3) Now compare the new estimate with the previous estimate and if they differ go back to the step labelled (2). If there is no difference, then the value of x is the square root of n.

In practice, rounding errors in the calculating device will sometimes cause successive estimates to differ in the last significant figure. In such cases, the process may be terminated by asking the question

$$|\text{previous estimate}-\text{latest estimate}| < d?$$

where d is a given small quantity.

Fig. 4 describes the process in flow-chart form, and fig. 5 shows the same process using algebraic symbols. The translation of the methods of this chapter into the basic language of chapter 2 is left as an exercise for the reader.

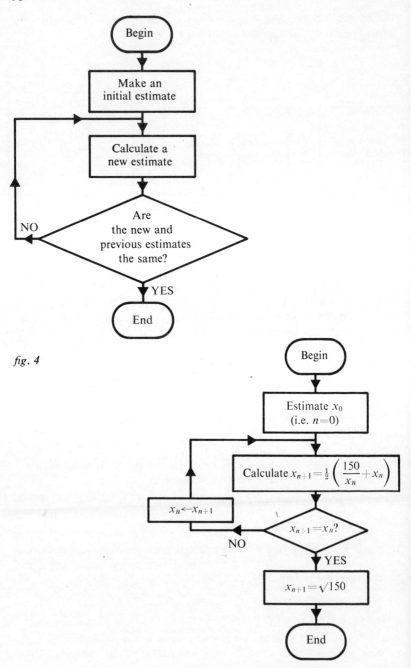

fig. 4

fig. 5

In fig. 5, the first estimate is denoted by x_0, and successive estimates by $x_1, x_2, \ldots, x_n, \ldots$ In the preceding example,

$$x_0 = 10$$
$$x_1 = 12 \cdot 5$$
$$x_2 = 12 \cdot 25$$
$$x_3 = 12 \cdot 25 \text{ (four sig. fig.).}$$

Each successive term of this sequence is given by the recurrence relation:

$$x_{n+1} = \frac{1}{2}\left(\frac{150}{x_n} + x_n\right).$$

The speed of the convergence can be shown by choosing a ridiculous first estimate (say 0·5) for $\sqrt{150}$. The results of the iterative process are shown in fig. 6.

n	x_n	$150/x_n$	$\frac{1}{2}\left(x_n + \dfrac{150}{x_n}\right)$
0	0·5	300	$\frac{1}{2}(300\cdot5) = 150\cdot3$
1	150·3	1·0	$\frac{1}{2}(151\cdot3) = 75\cdot7$
2	75·7	2·0	$\frac{1}{2}(77\cdot7) = 38\cdot9$
3	38·9	3·9	$\frac{1}{2}(42\cdot8) = 21\cdot4$
4	21·4	7·0	$\frac{1}{2}(28\cdot4) = 14\cdot2$
5	14·2	10·6	$\frac{1}{2}(24\cdot8) = 12\cdot4$
6	12·4	12·1	$\frac{1}{2}(24\cdot5) = 12\cdot25$
7	12·25	12·25	$\frac{1}{2}(24\cdot5) = 12\cdot25$

fig. 6

The above method involves long division only, and has the advantage of being 'self-correcting'. This means that should an error occur, the process will still converge on to the required value. In fig. 7, $\sqrt{17}$ is found, but an error is made when calculating the value of $\frac{1}{2}(4\cdot125 + 4\cdot121)$.

n	x_n	$17/x_n$	$\frac{1}{2}(x_n + 17/x_n)$
0	4	4·25	4·125
1	4·125	4·121	4·246 (error)
2	4·246	4·003	4·125
3	4·125	4·121	4·123
4	4·123	4·123	4·123

fig. 7

In automatic computing this sort of error is unlikely to occur, but it is an interesting point when considering the speed of convergence.

Not all numerical methods result in such rapid convergence and in practice some results will diverge. More will be said of divergent solutions later. It should also be pointed out that some results will oscillate. This could occur when the final print-out of a square root is given as:

1·7188
1·7189
1·7188
1·7189
.
.

etc.

In this case, rounding errors in the machine cause the last significant figure to oscillate between the values of 8 and 9. (The method given above shows how the iterative process may be terminated in this case.)

7.2 cube roots

A method for evaluating cube roots can be devised by treating the number, N, say, of which the cube root is required, as the volume of a rectangular solid. If this solid can be remoulded into a cube, then the edge of the cube will be the cube root of N. Given the value of N and a first estimate x as one edge of a rectangular solid, then N/x represents the area of the cross-section perpendicular to the edge of length x. If this cross-sectional area is assumed to be a square, then the length of the edges which bound the square face are $\sqrt{(N/x)}$. An iteration is now established by using this value as the next estimate for x.

Fig. 9 shows the results of the method when $N=8$ and x_0 is taken as 3. Fig. 10 shows the corresponding flow chart.

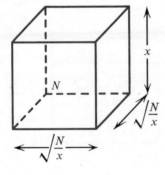

fig. 8

n	x_n	$8/x_n$	$x_{n+1}=\sqrt{(8/x_n)}$
0	3	2·67	1·63
1	1·63	4·91	2·22
2	2·22	3·60	1·90
3	1·90	4·21	2·05
4	2·05	3·90	1·97
5	1·97	4·06	2·01
6	2·01	3·98	2·00
7	2·00	4·00	2·00

fig. 9

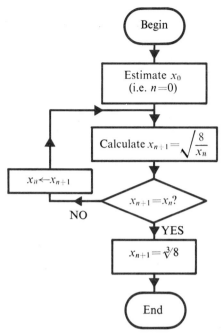

fig. 10

7.3 calculation of the zeros of polynomial functions

In this section, the computer is used to illustrate and extend the methods developed in *School Mathematics Project, Book 4*, chapter 2.

Consider the polynomial function:

$$f: x \to x^2 + 3x - 7.$$

The zeros of this function are the values of x in the solution set of the quadratic equation:

$$x^2 + 3x - 7 = 0.$$

A rearrangement of the equation in the form:

$$x^2 + 3x = 7$$
$$\Rightarrow x(x+3) = 7$$
$$\Rightarrow \frac{x+3}{7} = \frac{1}{x},$$

implies that there is a member x of the domain of the function f which has the same image under the two functions:

$$x \to \frac{x+3}{7},$$

$$\text{and} \quad x \to \frac{1}{x}.$$

In graphical terms, we require to find the values of x which correspond to the points of intersection of the graphs of these two functions. Fig. 11 shows that there are two intersections, and one lies between $x=1$ and $x=2$. We shall use an iterative technique to find this value of x more accurately.

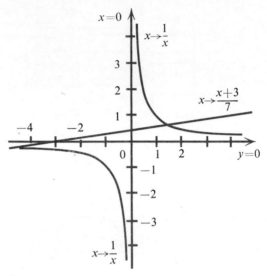

fig. 11

Using a first estimate of $x=1\cdot5$, we can calculate the value of the function $x\to(x+3)/7$. This value is then taken as a member of the range of the function $x\to1/x$, and the corresponding member of the domain of the function $x\to1/x$ is taken as our next estimate for the x coordinate of the required point of intersection.

Fig. 12 shows the procedure in tabular form, and fig. 13 gives the corresponding flow chart.

n	x_n	x_n+3	$\dfrac{x_n+3}{7}=\dfrac{1}{x_{n+1}}$	x_{n+1}
0	1·5	4·5	0·643	1·555
1	1·555	4·555	0·651	1·536
2	1·536	4·536	0·648	1·543
3	1·543	4·543	0·649	1·541
4	1·541	4·541	0·649	1·541

fig. 12

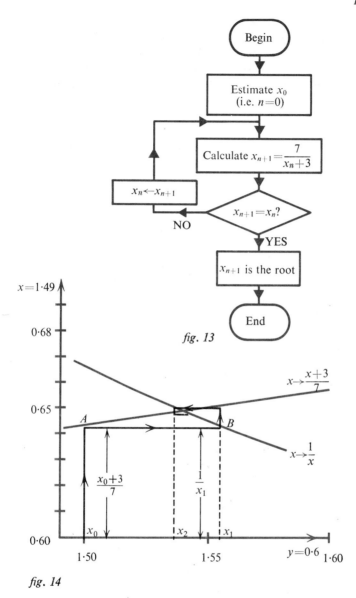

fig. 13

fig. 14

Fig. 14 shows the first three iterations of x on an enlarged section of the graphs of fig. 11. The first estimate, $x_0 = 1 \cdot 5$, is used to calculate the value of $(x_0 + 3)/7$ and this value is equated to $1/x_1$, to find the new estimate x_1. This transfer is shown in the figure by the horizontal line AB and the arrows indicate the path of the iteration. The new estimate, $x_1 = 1 \cdot 555$, is now used to calculate $(x_1 + 3)/7$, which leads to a new value for $1/x$ and hence for x.

What would have happened if the value of $1/x$ had been calculated first, and the transfer made in the opposite direction? Pupils should be encouraged to draw graphs of this situation and to discuss the following questions.

(a) What happens if our initial guess is higher than the value of x at the point of intersections?

(b) Could we have arranged the original function in a different way?

(c) Which method gives the greatest speed of convergence?

(d) Can we tell if a method is likely to diverge?

A fuller discussion of these points may be found in chapter 8 of *Practical Programming* (chapter 3, ref. 1), but the following examples illustrate the experimental approach to such problems.

example Find a zero value of the polynomial function $x \to x^2 - 10x - 1$ in the interval from $x=9$ to $x=10$.

The equation $x^2 - 10x + 1 = 0$ may be arranged in the form

$$x = 10 - \frac{1}{x}.$$

In this case, the iterative relation is $x_{n+1} = 10 - 1/x_n$. The results of a calculation using a first approximation of $x_0 = 9$ are given in fig. 15 and show a very rapid convergence.

n	x_n	$x_{n+1} = 10 - \dfrac{1}{x_n}$
0	9	$10 - 0 \cdot 111 = 9 \cdot 889$
1	$9 \cdot 889$	$10 - 0 \cdot 101 = 9 \cdot 899$
2	$9 \cdot 899$	$10 - 0 \cdot 101 = 9 \cdot 899$

fig. 15

Many pupils will be able to handle cubic functions and will want to find the zeros of these functions. The example given below is from the work of a class of fifteen- to sixteen-year-old boys and is presented in the way in which they tackled the problem. The figures given are from the print-out of an Olivetti Programma 101 which the class was using at the time.

example Show that the function $x \to x^3 + 4x^2 - 21$ has a zero value lying between $x=1$ and $x=2$. Assuming this value to be approximately $1 \cdot 89$, obtain its value to at least five decimal places.

$$f: x \to x^3 + 4x^2 - 21$$
$$\Rightarrow 1 \to -16$$

and $2 \to 3$.

Since the function changes sign between $x=1$ and $x=2$, there is a value of x between these values such that the function has a zero value.

Writing the equation as:

$$x^3 = 21 - 4x^2$$
$$\Rightarrow x = \frac{21}{x^2} - 4.$$

and following the procedure adopted for the quadratic, using $x_0 = 1 \cdot 89$, the Olivetti machine produced the figures given in fig. 16, whereupon the machine was stopped as the figures did not converge. An investigation into the graphs of

$$x \to x$$
$$\text{and} \quad x \to \frac{21}{x^2} - 4$$

demonstrates the non-convergence (fig. 17), the arrows indicating the direction of the attempted iteration.

n	x_n	$x_{n+1} = \dfrac{21}{x_n^2} - 4$
0	1·89	1·8788947677
1	1·8788947677	1·9485947123
2	1·9485947123	1·5306510153
3	1·5306510153	4·9632792480
4	4·9632792480	−3·1475245640
5	−3·1475245640	−1·8802675978
6	−1·8802675978	1·9399114496
7	1·9399114496	1·5802734621
8	1·5802734621	4·4092023078

fig. 16

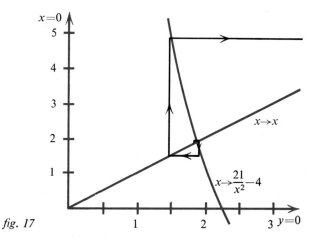

fig. 17

If the equation is rearranged in the form

$$x = +\sqrt{\frac{21}{4+x}},$$

and the functions $x \to x$ and $x \to +\sqrt{\frac{21}{4+x}}$

are graphed, it will be seen that by starting with $x_0 = 1 \cdot 8$, convergence takes place. The diagram is left as an exercise for the reader, but the output from the Olivetti obtained by the class mentioned earlier in this chapter is reproduced in fig. 18.

n	x_n	$x_{n+1} = \sqrt{\left(\dfrac{21}{4+x_n}\right)}$
0	1·8	1·90281098
1	1·90281098	1·88616728
2	1·88616728	1·88883206
3	1·88883206	1·88840465
4	1·88840465	1·88847319
5	1·88847319	1·88846219
6	1·88846219	1·88846396
7	1·88846396	1·88846397
8	1·88846397	1·88846372
9	1·88846372	1·88846371
10	1·88846371	1·88846371

fig. 18

7.4 calculation of the zeros of a function by the Bolzano method

We shall now investigate a procedure for calculating the zeros of polynomial functions which is similar to the methods described in section 7.1.

Consider $f : x \to x^3 - 2x - 5$

$$2 \to 8 - 4 - 5 = -1$$
$$3 \to 27 - 6 - 5 = 16$$

The function changes sign from negative to positive in the interval and hence there is a value of x between $x = 2$ and $x = 3$ such that $f(x)$ is zero at that point (fig. 19).

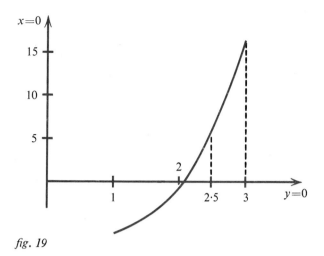

fig. 19

As in the square-root method, take the average of these two end points,

i.e. $x=\frac{1}{2}(2+3)=2\cdot5$

and evaluate the function for $x=2\cdot5$:

$2\cdot5\rightarrow(2\cdot5)^3-2(2\cdot5)-5$
$=15\cdot63-5-5$
$=5\cdot63$

It is now clear that the function has a zero value somewhere between $x=2$ and $x=2\cdot5$ and the process can be repeated by bisecting the interval $[2, 2\cdot5]$ and evaluating the function at $x=2\cdot25$.

$2\cdot25\rightarrow11\cdot39-4\cdot5-5$
$=11\cdot39-9\cdot5$
$=1\cdot89$

Again this is positive and so indicates that the graph of the function crosses $y=0$ between $x=2$ and $x=2\cdot25$.

Bisecting the interval $[2, 2\cdot25]$ gives $x=2\cdot13$ and

$2\cdot13\rightarrow9\cdot66-4\cdot26-5$
$=0\cdot40$

and we now know that the function has the value zero in the interval $[2, 2\cdot13]$. Repeat the process by evaluating the function at $x=\frac{1}{2}(2+2\cdot13)=2\cdot07$,

$2\cdot07\rightarrow8\cdot87-4\cdot14-5$
$=-0\cdot27$

The change in sign informs us that the zero of the function must now lie between $x=2\cdot07$ and $x=2\cdot13$ and thus we bisect the interval $[2\cdot07, 2\cdot13]$.

Clearly this process can go on until the desired degree of accuracy is obtained (the results of a computer output are shown in fig. 22); but first we shall give a generalisation of the process and the corresponding flow chart.

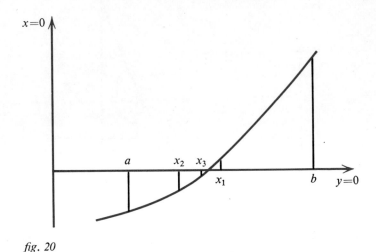

fig. 20

In general terms, we obtain an upper and a lower bound for the root of the equation, say $x=a$, $x=b$, so that our root lies in the interval $[a, b]$. Bisecting this interval to give x_1 as an upper bound we have the root in the interval $[a, x_1]$. In fig. 19 the mid-point of this interval, namely x_2, falls on the opposite side of the actual root from x_1 and so the next interval to be considered is $[x_2, x_1]$ and on the next cycle the interval becomes $[x_3, x_1]$.

N.B. So the process continues, but in order to standardise the procedure, as in the flow diagram, we shall assign the symbol a_n as the lower bound and b_n as the upper bound in order to calculate the mid-point x_{n+1} of that interval.

The details of the process are as follows:

(1) Let the value of the function at $x=a_0$ be negative and the value at $x=b_0$ be positive;

(2) Calculate x values according to the formula
$x_{n+1}=\frac{1}{2}(a_n+b_n)$;

(3) Evaluate the function, $f(x_{n+1})$ for this new valued x;

(4) If $x_{n+1}=x_n$ to the required degree of accuracy, then x_{n+1} is the value of x which makes the value of the function zero and is the root of the equation;

(5) If $x_{n+1}\neq x_n$ then test the sign of the value of the function evaluated in (3). If $f(x_{n+1})>0$, replace b_n by x_{n+1}, but if $f(x_{n+1})<0$, then replace a_n by x_{n+1} and go back to (2).

The flow chart for this process is shown in fig. 21.

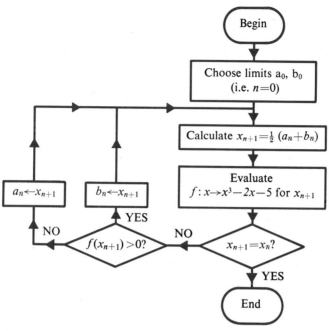

fig. 21

Fig. 22 shows the table of values for the iterative process.

n	a_n	b_n	x_{n+1}	$f(x_{n+1})$
0	2·00	3·00	2·50	5·63
1	2·00	2·50	2·25	1·89
2	2·00	2.25	2·13	0·40
3	2·00	2·13	2·07	−0·27
4	2·07	2·13	2·10	0·06
5	2·07	2·10	2·09	−0·05
6	2·09	2·10	2·09	−0·05

fig. 22

This is quite a long and tedious process, particularly when the value of x required is near to one of the bounds, as in the example given. The Egyptians used a method known as *reguli falsi* (the method of false position) which involves the ideas of linear interpolation, a process pupils may have met when using logarithm tables.

7.5 the method of false position

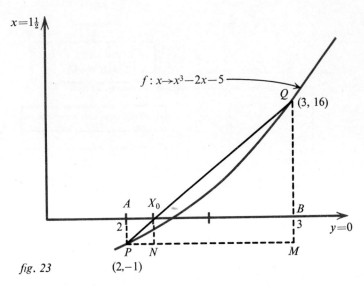

fig. 23

$f: x \to x^3 - 2x - 5.$

(2, −1)

We shall now investigate the method of false position using the function $f: x \to x^3 - 2x - 5$.

The values of the function corresponding to $x=2$ and $x=3$ suggest that the root is closer to 2 than to 3 (fig. 22) and this was, in fact, established for the function in the method of Bolzano.

By proportion, or the principle of enlargement, applied to the right-angled triangles PX_0N, PQM in fig. 23

$$\frac{PN}{PM} = \frac{MB}{MQ}$$

Let the straight line PQ intersect the line $y=0$ at X_0 and take the value of x at this point to be x_0.

Then

$$\frac{x_0 - 2}{1} = \frac{1}{17}$$
$$17(x_0 - 2) = 1$$
$$x_0 = \frac{35}{17} = 2 \cdot 06$$

The corresponding value of the function is

$$(2 \cdot 06)^3 - 2(2 \cdot 06) - 5$$
$$= 8 \cdot 74 - 4 \cdot 12 - 5$$
$$= -0 \cdot 38$$

The process can now be repeated using a lower bound at $(2 \cdot 06, -0 \cdot 38)$ – marked P_1 in fig. 24.

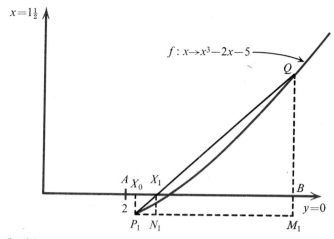

fig. 24

In fig. 24,
$$\frac{P_1N_1}{P_1M_1} = \frac{BM_1}{QM_1}.$$

Let X_1 have an x coordinate x_1. Then:
$$\frac{x_1 - 2 \cdot 06}{0 \cdot 94} = \frac{0 \cdot 38}{16 \cdot 38}$$

$$\Rightarrow 16 \cdot 38(x_1 - 2 \cdot 06) = 0 \cdot 38 \times 0 \cdot 94$$
$$\Rightarrow 16 \cdot 38 x_1 - 33 \cdot 74 = 0 \cdot 36$$
$$\Rightarrow \qquad 16 \cdot 38 x_1 = 34 \cdot 00$$
$$\Rightarrow \qquad x_1 = \frac{34 \cdot 00}{16 \cdot 38}$$
$$= 2 \cdot 08.$$

Repeating the process once more we have
$$\frac{x_2 - 2 \cdot 08}{0 \cdot 92} = \frac{0 \cdot 16}{16 \cdot 16}$$
$$\Rightarrow 16 \cdot 16 x_2 - 2 \cdot 08 \times 16 \cdot 16 = 0 \cdot 92 \times 0 \cdot 16$$
$$\Rightarrow \qquad 16 \cdot 16 x_2 = 33 \cdot 61 + 0 \cdot 15$$
$$\Rightarrow \qquad 16 \cdot 16 x_2 = 33 \cdot 76$$
$$\Rightarrow \qquad x_2 = \frac{33 \cdot 76}{16 \cdot 16} = 2 \cdot 09,$$

and so on. The drawing of a figure for each case is left to the reader.

Note that this method has converged much more rapidly; for here $x_2 = 2 \cdot 09$, whereas in the Bolzano method we had to go at least to x_5 for the same degree of accuracy.

All the methods discussed in this chapter are of an intuitive nature and are relatively simple to follow. The use of the calculus has been deliberately avoided and with the availability of a computer in the classroom much of the tedium of the arithmetic will have been taken away from the work, allowing the concept of an iterative process to stand out clearly.

examples

1   By writing $x^3-2x-5=0$ in the form

$$x=\sqrt{\left(\frac{5}{x}+2\right)}$$

obtain the root in the neighbourhood of $x=2$, correct to three decimal places.   [2·095]

2   Calculate the value of x in the region of 2·5 for which the function:

$$f: x \rightarrow 2x^3+x^2-33,$$

has a zero value.   [2·3896]

3   The function $f: x \rightarrow x^3+3x-7$ is zero in the region of $x=1·5$. Calculate this value of x correct to three decimal places.   [1·406]

4   The function $f: p \rightarrow 3p^3-9p+2$ has the value zero in the region $p=0·25$. Calculate this value of p correct to five decimal places.   [0·22607]

8 applications

8.1 area under a curve

The study of the area under a curve provides a wide variety of material of varying degree of difficulty. In the examples that follow, the knowledge of how to find the area of a trapezium is an essential preliminary.

examples A

1   Here are two flow charts; suggest shapes whose areas could be computed by using them. Are there other problems which could be solved using the same flow charts?

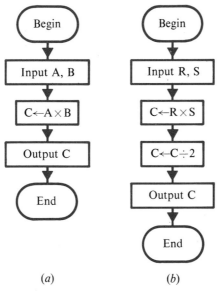

(a)   (b)

fig. 1

2   The parallel sides of a trapezium are *m* units and *r* units, and the distance between the parallel sides is *h* units. Write down the formula for the area of the trapezium, and then write out the flow chart.

If $m=4$ units, $r=6$ units and $h=3$ units, write out by the side of your flow chart the effect of each step of your flow chart using the units given. If the units are cm, what are the units of your answer?

3   In fig. 2, the area *B* has its two longer sides equal. Discuss the effect this has on **(a)** on its shape, and **(b)** on the flow chart for the trapezium. Can the same flow chart be used?

What has happened to the second of the 'parallel' sides in the shape *C*? Does this necessitate altering the flow chart? (No, 0 is the identity element under addition.)

Find the area of the given shape. (Use your flow chart for the trapezium to find the area of each strip and sum your results.)

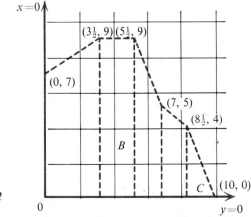

fig. 2

4   Plot the points P (3, $1\frac{1}{2}$), Q (1, 4), R (7, 6), S (6, 1). Put in the ordinates of P, Q, R, S. Now express the area of $PQRS$ as the difference between trapezia and hence calculate its area using your flow chart for the area of a trapezium.

5   Plot the points A (3, $2\frac{1}{3}$), B (1, 5), C (7, 7), D (9, 1). Try to find the area using the method given in question 4. What difficulties do you find? These can be avoided by putting in the abscissae of A, B, C, D and working from the base line $x=0$ instead of from $y=0$.

8.2 the area of a triangle

Triangle OPQ has its vertices at $(0, 0)$, (x_1, y_1), (x_2, y_2) as in fig. 3.

The area of triangle OPQ

$$=\text{triangle } OQM+\text{trapezium } QMNP-\text{triangle } ONP$$
$$=\tfrac{1}{2}x_2y_2+\tfrac{1}{2}(y_2+y_1)(x_1-x_2)-\tfrac{1}{2}x_1y_1$$
$$=\tfrac{1}{2}(x_1y_2-x_2y_1)$$

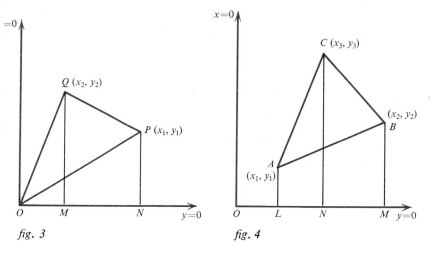

fig. 3

fig. 4

Write down the flow chart for this formula. Use your flow chart to find the areas of triangles with vertices:

a (0, 0), (2, 6), (4, 5); **b** (0, 0), (3, 3), (4, −5).

In fig. 4, the triangle ABC has vertices $A(x_1, y_1)$, $B(x_2, y_2)$, $C(x_3, y_3)$. AL, BM, CN are ordinates.

Triangle ABC

$$= \text{trapezium } ALNC + \text{trapezium } CNMB - \text{trapezium } ALMB$$
$$= \tfrac{1}{2}(y_3+y_1)(x_3-x_1) + \tfrac{1}{2}(y_2+y_3)(x_2-x_3) - \tfrac{1}{2}(y_2+y_1)(x_2-x_1)$$
$$= \tfrac{1}{2}[x_1(y_2-y_3) + x_2(y_3-y_1) + x_3(y_1-y_2)].$$

When using this formula take care to arrange that (x_1, y_1), (x_2, y_2), (x_3, y_3) circumscribe the triangle in an anti-clockwise direction to ensure that the area is positive. (Consider the signs of (y_2-y_3), (y_3-y_1), and (y_1-y_2).)

Write out the flow chart for this formula. Work through the flow chart to find the areas of triangles with vertices:

a (1, 3), (4, 1), (6, 8)
b (1, −2), (3, 3), (−3, 2)

Adapt your flow chart by inserting a counter so that the areas of n triangles with given coordinates could be found.

A figure has vertices (2, −2), (5, 1), (3, 7), (−2, 6), (−3, −1). Divide the figure into triangles and use the adapted flow chart to find its area.

8.3 the trapezium rule

So far we have considered areas where the outline is composed of straight-line segments. If we consider an area such as that shown in the diagram (fig. 5), an estimate of the area can be obtained by dividing it up into strips each of which is approximately a trapezium. At first sight it might seem sensible to be guided by the outline of the graph and have strips of varying width, but strips of equal width make for quicker calculation.

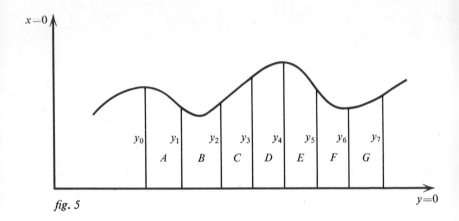

fig. 5

Divide the area into strips of equal width, e.g. seven strips. Call the lengths of the ordinates y_0, y_1, y_2, y_3, y_4, y_5, y_6, y_7. (With seven strips there are eight ordinates, and it helps pupils to have the last suffix the same as the number of strips.)

Let the width of each strip be d units.

$$\text{area of trapezium } A = \tfrac{1}{2}(y_0+y_1) \times d$$
$$\text{area of trapezium } B = \tfrac{1}{2}(y_1+y_2) \times d$$
$$\text{area of trapezium } C = \tfrac{1}{2}(y_2+y_3) \times d$$
$$\text{area of trapezium } D = \tfrac{1}{2}(y_3+y_4) \times d$$
$$\text{area of trapezium } E = \tfrac{1}{2}(y_4+y_5) \times d$$
$$\text{area of trapezium } F = \tfrac{1}{2}(y_5+y_6) \times d$$
$$\text{area of trapezium } G = \tfrac{1}{2}(y_6+y_7) \times d$$

Whole area under curve

$$\simeq \tfrac{1}{2}d[(y_0+y_7)+2(y_1+y_2+y_3+y_4+y_5+y_6)].$$

Why is this only an approximation to the area? Look at trapezium E and trapezium F. How many areas are too small? Are any areas too large? Could we obtain a better approximation to the area under the curve by increasing the number of strips? What changes would this necessitate in the formula? With n strips the formula becomes:

$$A = \tfrac{1}{2}d[(y_0+y_n)+2(y_1+y_2 \ldots +y_{n-1})]$$

The flow chart in fig. 6 uses the formula:

$$A = d[\tfrac{1}{2}(y_0 + y_n) + (y_1 + y_2 \ldots + y_{n-1})]$$

It is assumed that the ordinates y_i are already known.

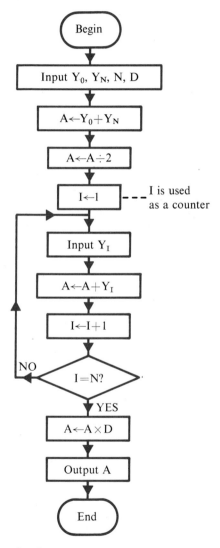

fig. 6

118

8.4 the approximate area of a circle

Construct a quadrant of a circle of radius ten cm. Divide the area into ten strips of one cm width.

    a Make each strip into a rectangle using the longer side of each strip as the long side of the rectangle. Find the sum of the areas of these rectangles. (Use fig. 6.)

    b Make each strip into a rectangle using the shorter side of each strip as the long side of the rectangle. Find the sum of the areas of these rectangles. (Use fig. 6.)

Complete the statement:

$$a < \text{area of quadrant} < b,$$

putting in the values of a and b. Between what values must the area of the whole circle lie? What would be the area of a square drawn on the radius of the circle? Find $4a$ and $4b$, and the ratio of $4a$ to r^2, and the ratio of $4b$ to r^2.

Calculate the area of the circle using the trapezium rule. Explain why this is a better estimate of the area. Find the ratio of the area to the area of the square on the radius.

Draw a number of circles of different radii, then use the trapezium rule to find their areas. In each case find the ratio of the area to the square on the radius. (This can be used either to suggest a formula for the area of a circle, or to find an approximation for π.)

8.5 area of an ellipse (see fig. 7)

Tie a piece of strong thread to two pins so that the length of thread between the pins is 18 cm. Mark two points A and B, 5 cm apart, with A near the left-hand edge of the paper. Stick the pins in at A and B. Put a pencil in the loop of the string, and, keeping the string taut, draw the resulting locus. This is one way to construct an ellipse. Only a quarter of the whole ellipse need be drawn. Use AB produced as $y=0$, and the perpendicular bisector of AB as $x=0$. The semi-major axis of the ellipse is OR and OT is the semi-minor axis. Measure OR and OT and evaluate $OR \times OT$.

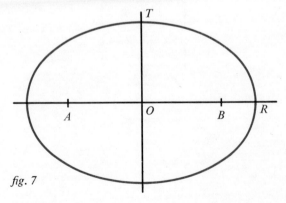

fig. 7

Calculate the area of a quadrant of this ellipse by dividing the quadrant into strips of width 1 cm and using your trapezium rule flow chart to find the approximate area. Find the ratio of the area of the whole ellipse to the product of the axes. Suggest a formula for the area of an ellipse. What shape would the ellipse have if the axes were equal? Do you think your suggested formula for the area of an ellipse is correct?

8.6 examples of areas which represent physical quantities

examples B

1 Fig. 8 shows the water consumption of a mill. What does a unit of area represent? Suggest possible explanations for the shape. Use the flow chart prepared in question 2, examples A, to estimate the total consumption.

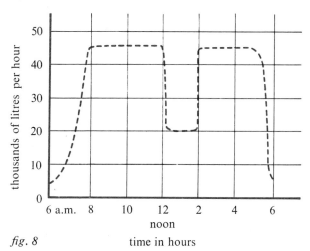

fig. 8   time in hours

2 The speed of a car in metres per second at intervals of one second is shown in the following table:

time in seconds	0	1	2	3	4	5	6	7	8	9	10
speed in metres per second	3	5	9	12	20	16	10	6	5	4	0

Draw the graph. Use the flow chart for the trapezium rule to compute:

  a the distance gone in the first four seconds,
  b the distance gone in the first six seconds,
  c the total distance gone.

Deduce the distance gone between the fourth and sixth seconds, and the average speed during the ten seconds.

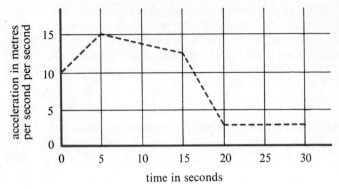

fig. 9

3 Fig. 9 shows the acceleration of a vehicle in metres per second per second during thirty seconds. If the speed at the beginning of the time shown was 30 m s^{-1} find the speed at the end of the thirty seconds.

4 Fig. 10 shows the consumption of gas in litres per minute in a block of flats. Account for the shape of the graph. Compute the total volume of gas used in one day. (Look at the units on the axes carefully.)

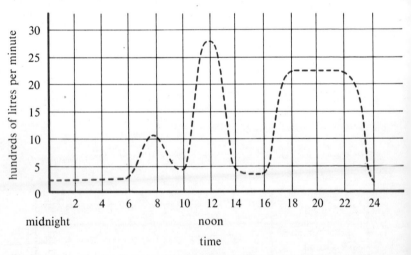

fig. 10

examples C Use the flow chart in fig. 6 in the following questions.

1 Find the area between the graphs of $y=x$, $y=0$, $x=0$, $x=4$ using forty strips. Compare your result with x^2 when $x=4$.

2 Find the area between the graphs of $y=x^2$, $y=0$, $x=0$, $x=3$ using thirty strips. Compare your result with x^3 when $x=3$.

3   Use twenty strips to find the area between $y=x^3$, $y=0$, $x=0$, $x=2$. Compare with x^4 when $x=2$.

4   What would you expect the area between $y=x^4$, $y=0$, $x=0$, $x=2$, to be? Use forty strips to find the area. Was your guess approximately correct?

5   Draw the graph of $y=x(x-2)$, between $x=0$ and $x=3$. The line $y=0$ divides the area into two parts. Using strips $1/10$ unit wide, find the area of the two parts. What is the total area?

8.7 further areas

So far the calculation of the values of the ordinates has not presented much difficulty, but it is time consuming. It is a great advantage to arrange to have within the flow chart a subroutine to calculate the required values.

Suppose we require the area between $y=1/(1+x^2)$, $y=0$, $x=x_0$, $x=x_n$, where n is the number of strips.

Fig. 11 shows the flow chart.

examples D

1   Sketch the graph of $y=1/x$ for values of x from $\frac{1}{2}$ to 10. Find the area between the graph and $y=0$, $x=1$, $x=3$. Use twenty strips and adapt the flow chart in fig. 11. (Compare your result with $\log_e 3$.)

2   Adapt fig. 11 to find the area between $y=4/(1+x^2)$, $y=0$, $x=0$, $x=1$. Compare your result with π.

3   Repeat question 2, but with $y=\sqrt{(1-x^2)}$. It will be noticed that this curve is a quadrant of a circle, centre the origin and of radius 1 unit. Compare your calculated value with one-quarter of the theoretical area of this circle.

4   Radian measure is needed for this question (see chapter 3, Ex. A.). Find the area between the graph of the mapping $x \rightarrow \cos x$, for values of x from 0 to $\pi/2$, using nine strips. Compare with the value of $\sin \pi/2$. From the area calculated in the first part of the question, deduce the area between $y=\cos x$, $y=0$, $x=0$, $x=\pi$.

5   Radian measure again. Find the area between $x=0$, $x=\pi$, $y=0$, and also:

a $y=\cos^2 x$,
b $y=\sin^2 x$.

Use twenty strips in each case. What is the sum of these areas?

6   Sketch the graph of $y=x$ for values of x from 0 to 2. Find

a the area between the graph, the lines $x=0$, $y=2$ using twenty strips parallel to $y=0$, and
b the area between the graph, the lines $y=0$, $x=2$ using twenty strips parallel to $x=0$. Add the results of **a** and **b**. Interpret your result.

122

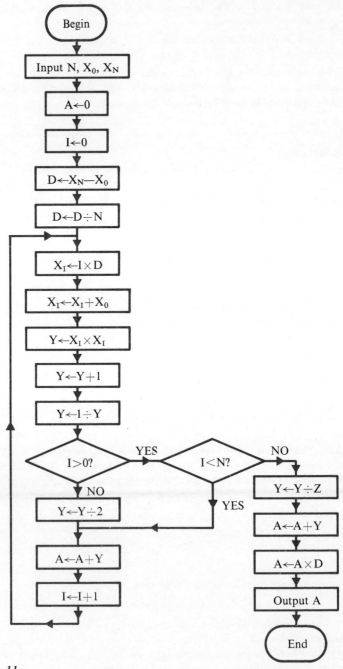

fig. 11

8.8 an application to statistics (A flow chart to construct a frequency diagram.)

Suppose a dairy wished to display information about the number of customers who take no milk, one pint, two pints, three pints, etc., on any one day. Fig. 12 gives a flow chart for sorting the information.

  n is the total number of customers;
  i the number of customers so far considered;
  r is the contents of a counter;
  p is the number of pints taken by the customer under consideration;
  a is the number of customers so far considered who had no milk;
  b is the number of customers so far considered who had one pint;
  c is the number of customers so far considered who had two pints, etc.

After a particular set of information has been sorted, a frequency diagram may be constructed, and the flow chart in fig. 6 used to find its area. What would the area of this frequency diagram represent?

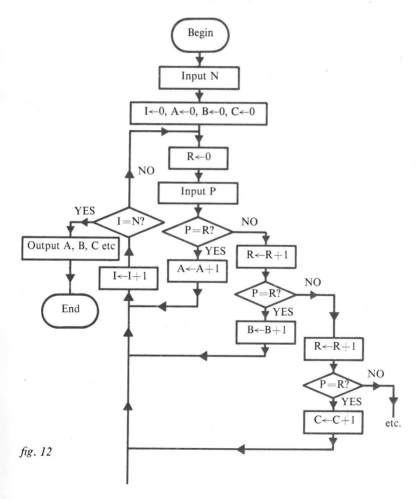

fig. 12

Statistics about themselves are always a source of interest to pupils. Some suggestions are: shoe sizes, pocket money, distance travelled to school.

If the cumulative frequency curve is drawn below the frequency diagram, using the same horizontal scale, the relation between the parts into which the frequency diagram is divided by the median and quartiles can be shown (see *School Mathematics Project, Book 3*). Mark the positions of the quartiles and median on the cumulative frequency curve and by mapping from the cumulative frequency curve on to the frequency diagram, mark the quartiles and median on the frequency diagram. Find, using the flow chart in fig. 6,

a the areas of the two parts into which the median divides the frequency diagram,

b the areas of the four parts into which the quartiles divide the frequency diagram.

8.9 the solution of linear equations

Usually methods for solving two linear equations, as taught in schools, lead to exact rational solutions. The general theme of chapter 7 was to consider iterative processes for calculating values of the variables that lead to approximate zero values of the functions.

We shall now investigate an iterative method for solving the equations:

$$5x+3y=6, \tag{1}$$
$$4x+7y=8. \tag{2}$$

(1) may be solved to give x in terms of y;

$$\text{i.e. } x=(6-3y)/5, \tag{3}$$

(2) similarly gives

$$y=(8-4x)/7. \tag{4}$$

We shall now make an estimate for our values of x and y and use these estimates in (3) and (4) to obtain the next values of x and y. Let us assume that $x_0=0$ and $y_0=0$, clearly ridiculous assumptions if we draw the two lines on a graph. However, throughout chapter 7 we discovered that we were able to make such wild guesses and yet arrive at good solutions.

In (3) $x_1=(6-0)/5=1\cdot20$ (two decimal places)
In (4) $y_1=(8-0)/7=1\cdot14$

These values may now be used to calculate x_2 and y_2:

$$x_2=(6-3\times1\cdot14)/5=(6-3\cdot42)/5$$
$$=(2\cdot58)/5$$
$$=0\cdot52$$
$$y_2=(8-4\times1\cdot20)/7=(8-4\cdot80)/7$$
$$=(3\cdot20)/7$$
$$=0\cdot46.$$

This process is continued in tabulated form in fig. 13 in which the convergence of the solution is clearly shown.

The solution to equations (1) and (2) is, correct to two decimal places:

$x=0.78$, $y=0.70$.

n	x_n	y_n
0	0	0
1	1·20	1·14
2	0·52	0·46
3	0·92	0·85
4	0·69	0·62
5	0·83	0·75
6	0·75	0·67
7	0·79	0·71
8	0·77	0·69
9	0·79	0·70
10	0·78	0·69
11	0·79	0·70

fig. 13

It should be noticed that the table shows that the solutions oscillate. This is because the calculations have all been rounded to two significant figures.

The process just described will only give a solution when the equations are arranged in the order in which they were given at the beginning. Thus if we interchange the equations and write them as

$$4x+7y=8 \tag{1}$$
$$\text{and} \quad 5x+3y=6 \tag{2}$$
$$\text{we get} \quad x=(8-7y)/4 \tag{3}$$
$$\text{and} \quad y=(6-5x)/3 \tag{4}$$

Repeating the steps of the first attempt by putting $x_0=0$ and $y_0=0$ leads to $x_1=2$, $y_1=2$. Further values of x_n, y_n are given in fig. 14.

n	x_n	y_n
0	0	0
1	2·00	2·00
2	−1·50	−1·33
3	4·33	4·50
4	−5·88	−5·22
5	11·14	11·80
.	.	.
.	.	.

fig. 14

There is a simple rule which will ensure that the equations are arranged in the correct order for convergence to take place, but the proof is beyond the scope of this book (ref. 1). The simple rule is to order the equations

$$a_1x+b_1y+c_1=0 \tag{5}$$
$$a_2x+b_2y+c_2=0 \tag{6}$$

in a way such that

$$|a_1b_2|>|a_2b_1|$$

where $|a_1b_2|$ means the *numerical* value of a_1b_2.

Applying this to the pair of equations used above, in the first attempt we have $|a_1b_2|=35$ and $|a_2b_1|=12$ and since $35>12$ the estimates will converge to a solution.

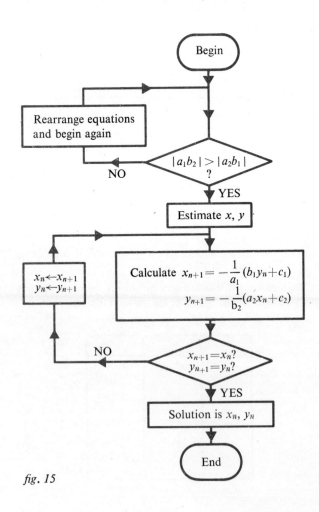

fig. 15

The flow chart of the process is given in fig. 15, starting from the equations in the form of (5) and (6) above.

Since the above process requires several iterations to obtain a solution, it is worth while looking for a faster process. Such a method is to consider putting $x_0=0$ only, using this value of x_0 to calculate y_0 in one of the equations and following this up by using the y_0 (calculated) to find x_1 in the other equation.

For the equations:

$$5x+3y=6,$$
$$4x+7y=8,$$

in the form:

$$x=(6-3y)/5,$$
$$y=(8-4x)/7,$$

we obtain:

$$x_0=0, \quad y_0=(8-4\times0)/7=1\cdot14$$
$$\text{and,} \quad x_1=(6-3\times1\cdot14)/5=(2\cdot58)/5=0\cdot52.$$

This value of x_1 can now be used to compute y_1 (cf. the previous method when x_0 was used to calculate y_1).

The table of the iterative solution is given in fig. 16.

The graphical representation of the solution is given in fig. 17 and the successive points in the iterative process are clearly seen. It is of interest to follow

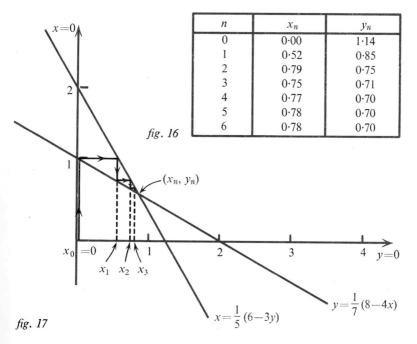

n	x_n	y_n
0	0·00	1·14
1	0·52	0·85
2	0·79	0·75
3	0·75	0·71
4	0·77	0·70
5	0·78	0·70
6	0·78	0·70

fig. 16

fig. 17

this work by attempting this quicker method on the two equations:

$$5x+3y=6,$$
$$4x+7y=8,$$

when arranged in the form:

$$x=(8-7y)/4,$$
$$y=(6-5x)/3.$$

Let $x_0=0$, then $y_0=(6-0)/3=2$, $x_1=\frac{1}{4}(8-14)=-1\cdot5$,

$y_1=(6+7\cdot5)/3=4\cdot5$, etc.

Fig. 18 demonstrates that the successive results are diverging. This is shown even more dramatically in fig. 19.

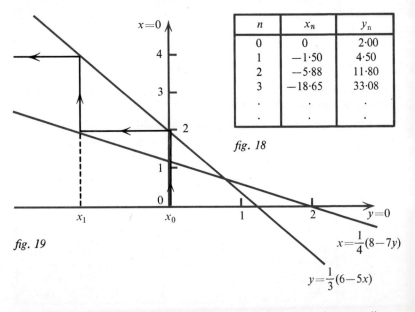

n	x_n	y_n
0	0	2·00
1	−1·50	4·50
2	−5·88	11·80
3	−18·65	33·08
.	.	.
.	.	.

fig. 18

fig. 19

$$x=\frac{1}{4}(8-7y)$$

$$y=\frac{1}{3}(6-5x)$$

The second method given above can be extended to more than two linear equations. Try to solve the equations:

$$4x+y+2z=4,$$
$$3x+8y-z=20,$$
$$2x-y-4z=4.$$

Rewriting these as:

$$x=(4-y-2z)/4 \qquad (1)$$
$$y=(20-3x+z)/8 \qquad (2)$$
$$z=-(4+y-2x)/4 \qquad (3)$$

and assuming $y_0=z_0=0$ we have

$$x_1=(4-0-2\cdot0)/4=1 \text{ (from equation (1))}.$$

In (2), with the values $x_1=1$, $z_0=0$ we calculate:

$$y_1=(20-3\cdot1+0)/8=2\cdot125,$$

and rounding this to $2\cdot13$ we can proceed to calculate x_n, y_n, z_n using the most up-to-date values of two of the variables to calculate the third.

Thus:

$$z_1=-(4+2\cdot13-2)/4=1\cdot03.$$

The successive values of x_n, y_n and z_n are given in fig. 20.

n	x_n	y_n	z_n
0		0	0
1	1·00	2·13	−1·03
2	0·98	2·00	−1·01
3	1·00	2·00	−1·00
4	1·00	2·00	−1·00

fig. 20

The solutions are therefore:

$$x=1\cdot00 \quad y=2\cdot00 \quad z=-1\cdot00$$

Once again the convergence of the solutions of these equations is only possible if certain conditions hold in so far as the arrangement of the equations is concerned. For the sake of completeness the conditions necessary for convergence will be stated.

For the equations:

$$a_1x+b_1y+c_1z+d_1=0$$
$$a_2x+b_2y+c_2z+d_2=0$$
$$a_3x+b_3y+c_3z+d_3=0,$$

they will only converge to a solution if:

$$|a_1|\geqslant|b_1|+|c_1|$$
$$|b_2|\geqslant|a_2|+|c_2|$$
$$|c_3|\geqslant|a_3|+|b_3|$$

but limited to the criterion that *at least* one of these statements must be confined to the inequality.

Thus for the equations we have solved:

$$a_1=4 \quad b_1=1 \quad c_1=2$$
and $|4|$ is greater than $|1|+|2|$
$$a_2=3 \quad b_2=8 \quad c_2=-1$$
and $|8|$ is greater than $|3|+|-1|$
$$a_3=2 \quad b_3=-1 \quad c_3=-4$$
and $|-4|$ is greater than $|2|+|-1|$

Thus all three statements are satisfied and the equations should converge to a solution.

examples E Test the following equations for convergence (it may be necessary to rearrange some of them) and if they can be made to converge, obtain the solution correct to two decimal places.

1 $3x-4y=-1$
   $5x+y=6$
   $\begin{bmatrix} x=1{\cdot}00 \\ y=1{\cdot}00 \end{bmatrix}$

2 $2x-y=1$
   $x+3y=-17$
   $\begin{bmatrix} x=-2{\cdot}00 \\ y=-5{\cdot}00 \end{bmatrix}$

3 $7x+2y-3z=1$
   $x-5y-2z=6$
   $-x+y+4z=8$
   $\begin{bmatrix} x=2{\cdot}00 \\ y=-2{\cdot}00 \\ z=3{\cdot}00 \end{bmatrix}$

references

chapter 1 basic concepts
1 *From Abacus to Addo.* G. N. Porter. (Addo Ltd)
2 *The Japanese Abacus explained.* Y. Yoshino. (Dover)
3 *Mathematics Teaching.* Summer 1965, number 31. (A.T.M.)
4 *School Mathematics with the Desk Calculator.* W. D. Lewis. (Heinemann)
5 *Man and Computer; A Perspective* (film), IBM United Kingdom Ltd, 389 Chiswick High Road, London, W.4.
6 *Some Lessons in Mathematics.* A.T.M. (C.U.P.)
7 *Matrices 1.* G. Matthews. (Arnold)
8 *The Gentle Art of Mathematics.* D. Pedoe. (Penguin)
9 *School Mathematics Project, Book 3.* (C.U.P.)
10 *Pattern and Power of Mathematics 4.* Moakes, Croome, Phillips. (Macmillan)
11 *School Mathematics Project. Additional Maths, Book 2.* (C.U.P.)
12 *New Mathematics Pamphlet 2.* Snell, Morgan, Parsonson, Bloxham. (C.U.P.)
13 *Further Exercises in Modern Mathematics.* D. Marjoram. (Pergamon)
14 *School Mathematics Project, Advanced Book 1.* (C.U.P.)
15 *Maths Today.* Autumn Term, Year 1. (B.B.C.)

chapter 2 the computer
1 Described in *Computer Education.* December 1970.
2 School Mathematics Project handbook, *Practical Programming.* Corlett and Tinsley. (C.U.P.)
3 *School Mathematics Project, Advanced Books 1-4.* (C.U.P.)
4 *School Mathematics Project, Book 3*, chapter 14;
School Mathematics Project, Book 4, chapter 15. (C.U.P.)

chapter 3 elements of programming
1 School Mathematics Project handbook, *Practical Programming.* Corlett and Tinsley, (C.U.P.)
2 *1900 Fortran (Programmed Text).* (I.C.L.)
3 *A guide to Algol programming.* McCracken. (Wiley)
4 *A guide to Fortran programming.* McCracken. (Wiley)
5 See page 66 of ref. 1

chapter 8 applications
1 *Numerical methods and Fortran programming.* McCracken and Dorn. (Wiley)

index

absolute error, 55, 56
accumulator, in computer, 20
Achilles and the tortoise, 87–8
addition of approximate numbers, errors in, 56–8
algebra, basic: for flow charts and programs, 25–8
Algol programming language, 21
area: of circle, 118; of ellipse, 118–19; representing physical quantity, 119–21; of trapezium, 113–14; of triangle, 114–15; under a curve, 113–14
arithmetic progression, 89–93
arithmetic unit (processor), in computer, 2, 3, 18
associative law, 25

binary arithmetic, 8, 9; cyclically permuted, 7; transition from decimal to, in computer, 18
binomial theorem, 60
Bolzano method for calculating zeros of polynomial functions, 106–9

calculating devices, 1; accuracy of, 51
calculus, 64, 82
chess, program for game of, 48
circle, area of, 118
Cobol programming language, 21
combinations, 75
compiler, for transcribing programming languages into machine code, 21
complement, 9; subtraction by adding, 8–9

compound interest, 94
computer, basic concept of, 1–2
computer game, 2–4, 17
control unit, in computer, 2, 3, 19
convergence: conditions for, in solution of linear equations by iterative method, 125–6, 128, 129, 130
convergent sequence, 79
convergent series, 88, 92–3
cost, of computing by hand and by machine, 16
counter, in computer, 5, 34–5
cube roots, by iterative method, 100–1
cubic functions, calculation of zeros of, 104
curve, calculation of area under, 113–14
cylinder, volume of, 27–8

data: exact and inexact, 51; false, 35; processing of, 44
de-bugging of translated program, 25
decision elements, in computer programs, 18, 20, 23–4, 32
distributive law, 25
divergent sequence, 79
divergent series, 92
division: of approximate numbers, errors in, 60–1; by zero, to be avoided, 25, 32
draughts, program for game of, 48

e, series convergent to, 93
ellipse, area of, 118–19